OSPREY MILITARY JOURNAL

VOLUME 2 • ISSUE 3

page 6

page 23

page 47

Contents

Published by Osprey Publishing Limited

Editorial
Editors: William Shepherd and Marcus Cowper

Advertising
North America: Carl A. Smith, P.O. Box 2765, Manassas VA 20108 USA
Tel: (703) 365-0159 • Fax: (703) 365-9691 • E-mail: carlsmithjr@prodigy.net
UK/Europe/International: Joanna Sharland, Osprey Publishing Ltd,
Elms Court, Chapel Way, Botley, Oxford OX2 9LP, UK
Tel: 01865 727022 • Fax: 01865 727017
• E-mail: info@ospreypublishing.com

Circulation/Distribution
North America: Osprey USA, 443 Park Avenue South,
Suite 800, New York, NY 10016, USA
Tel: (212) 685-5560 • Fax: (212) 685-5836 • E-mail: ospreyusa@aol.com
UK/Europe/International: Osprey Publishing Ltd, Elms Court,
Chapel Way, Botley, Oxford OX2 9LP, UK
Tel: 01865 727022 • Fax: 01865 727017
• E-mail: info@ospreypublishing.com

Osprey Military Journal (ISSN 1467-1379) is published bi-monthly by
Osprey Publishing Limited. Subscription rates for one year (six issues)
US & Canada $39.95 US; UK £25.50; Europe £33.50; rest of world £42.50
Periodicals postage paid.

Subscription enquiries/address changes
North America: Osprey Direct USA, PO Box 130, Sterling Hts,
MI 48311-0130 Tel: (810) 795-2763 • Fax: (810) 795-4266
E-mail: info@ospreydirectusa.com
UK/Europe/International: Osprey Direct UK, PO Box 140,
Wellingborough, Northants NN8 4ZA, UK
Tel: 01933 443863 • Fax: 01933 443849 • E-mail: info@ospreydirect.co.uk

Design: Active Designs, Oxon, UK
Origination: Grasmere Digital Imaging, Leeds, UK
Printed in the UK by Stones the Printers, Banbury, Oxon, UK

Front Cover *The allied Oda/Tokugawa army take a brief rest on their way to the relief of Nagashino. On the left is one of Tokugawa Ieyasu's elite messengers engaged in conversation with Sakakibara Yasumasa. Shielding his eyes from the sun is Sakai Tadatsugu, another Tokugawa retainer. Behind them the Tokugawa army marches on. (© 2000, Osprey Publishing Ltd., illustration by Howard Gerrard from Campaign 69 Nagashino 1575)*

Editorial

This Issue marks two important anniversaries. 60 years ago, in May 1940, the German army swept through Belgium and France to the English Channel. Major Tom Mouat tells the full story of the capture of the immensely strong and sophisticated fortress of Eben Emael, assessing the effectiveness of the secret new ordnance that was to be the tiny assault team's key weapon. Looking at the final days of that extraordinary month, Martin Marix Evans investigates the different reasons given for the delay in the Panzers' final assault on Dunkirk and comes up with a new and persuasive account of the leadership and intelligence factors that were critical to the German high command's decision-making. Europe's south-western coastline was the main scene for the longer conflict between Viking and Moor; Dr David Nicolle tells how superior sea and land power set the limits to Viking expansion on the Iberian peninsular and in the western Mediterranean. Stephen Turnbull, the leading western authority on the history of the Samurai, picks up on the theme of weaponry and fortification in an account, based on his own research, of the evolution of Japanese defensive engineering and architecture through the 16th century, in line with the increasing effectiveness of firepower. A century later and in the Americas, leadership, and also discipline in the ranks, were key factors in the success of the buccaneer Henry Morgan's march across the isthmus and raid on the city of Panama; Angus Konstam, former curator of the Mel Fisher Maritime Heritage Center follows the buccaneers on campaign. Finally, René Chartrand continues Osprey's celebration of the battle of Marengo, the second anniversary in the Issue, with a historical investigation of the famous dish named after the battle and offers a delicious recipe for re-enactment.

William Shepherd   Marcus Cowper

The Error that lost the War?

Hitler's Halt Order 24 May 1940

MARTIN MARIX EVANS

Tank country; 1st Panzer Regiment, Gruppe Guderian, advances, June 1940. (B80/32/30A)

As the French and British stumbled back across the fields of Flanders and the Panzer divisions pushed up from the south, an order was sent from German Army Group A headquarters at Charleville-Mézières to the commanders at the front. It was conveyed by telephone at 12.31pm on 24 May. The order was as follows:

At the Führer's orders the attack to the east of Arras with VIII and II Corps, in co-operation with the left wing of Army Group B, is to be continued towards the northwest. On the other hand, forces advancing to the northwest of Arras are not to go beyond the general line Lens-Béthune-Aire-St Omer-Gravelines (Canal Line). On the west wing, all mobile units are to close up and let the enemy throw himself against the above-mentioned favourable defensive line.

This was the famous 'Halt Order'. It came as a shock to General Heinz Guderian, in command of XIX Panzer Corps which was thrusting up the coast of the English Channel past Boulogne and Calais. It came as a welcome relief to Generalmajor Erwin Rommel. It came as a blessing to the hard-pressed British Expeditionary Force and their French allies. From the middle of Friday 24 May until the early afternoon of Sunday 26 May the order remained in force and the Panzers stood still, and when the order was lifted it took time to get moving again, so two and a half days were granted to the Allies in which to organise the defence of Dunkirk, from the beachheads of which nearly 200,000 British and 140,000 of their allies would escape.

It is not surprising that the Halt Order has been the subject of speculation and that various explanations, including the braggodocio of Reichsmarshall Herman Göring and the back-seat driving of Adolf Hitler, have been advanced for it. It has been suggested that Göring pressed Hitler to give the Luftwaffe the honour of destroying the British at Dunkirk. Another possibility put forward is that fear of the Flanders mud made Hitler hold back his tanks. The 'Golden Bridge' idea, the possibility that Hitler deliberately gave the British the chance to escape, has also been mooted. And, finally, it is said that Hitler over-ruled everyone and quite simply failed to appreciate the opportunity before him.

AN ALLIED VIEW

On 10 May the Germans had launched their offensive.

In accordance with the prudent provisions of Plan D, the French and British had advanced to lines of defence in Belgium to forestall the obvious enemy thrust through the Low Countries and across the French border to strike at Paris.

Now, a mere fortnight later, the BEF and the French 1st Army had been cut off and, together with the rapidly weakening Belgian Army, was beset by the mighty, mechanised monster that had sliced through France so effortlessly while the skies were riven with their screaming dive-bombers. Or so it appeared.

How could one resist? General Gaston Billotte, commanding No.1 Army Group and to whom Lord Gort of the BEF reported, could only remark:

Je suis crevé de fatigue – et contre ces Panzers je ne peux rien faire. [I am exhausted – and I can do nothing against these Panzers].

The ground was thoroughly prepared for popular myth-making.

THE GERMAN VIEW

Although their advance had seemed to the Allies some sort of juggernaut, hearts were in German mouths. The southerly strike by XIX Panzer Corps under Guderian had been a worrying business. After getting over the Meuse at Sedan, Guderian had persuaded his Group Commander, General Ewald von Kleist, that it would be wise to move on a bit to allow supporting formations to cross the river and was given leave to keep moving for twenty-four hours. He then left 10th Panzer and the Grossdeutschland Regiment to deal with the French threat to the south of the Sedan salient at Stonne and shot off westwards. On 15 May he was over

the Ardennes Canal. On that day Rundstedt's fears were recorded in the Army Group A War Diary, speculating on the possibility of having to halt on the River Oise lest the French attack from the Aisne or in the Laon region. By the morning of 17 May Guderian was 30 miles (50km) away ready to leave Montcornet, northeast of Laon, and

head for St Quentin. Kleist was not only angry but scared; the southern flank was terribly vulnerable and he hurried off to confront his over-enthusiastic subordinate. With Guderian offering his resignation and Kleist accepting it, only the intervention of Colonel-general List prevented Guderian's abdication of his command. That same afternoon Hitler

Infantry Tank A12, Matilda Mark I Gamecock, 7th Bn., RTR, 1st Army Tank Bde., BEF; France, 1940. (© Osprey Publishing Ltd., from New Vanguard 8: Matilda Infantry Tank 1938-1945 by David Fletcher, illustration by Peter Sarson)

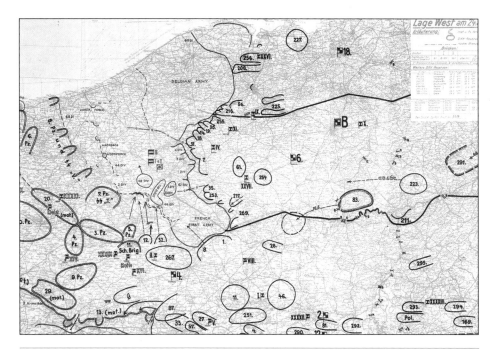

The German situation map for 25 May 1940 shows how Army Group A was spread thinly from Sedan to the Channel, giving grounds for fears of Allied attacks from the south and casting doubt on the army's ability to crush the Allies in Flanders. (HMSO)

visited Rundstedt's headquarters in Bastogne, having vented his apprehensions on the staff of OKW (Armed Forces High Command) earlier in the day. His fears for the southern flank were also vivid.

The flank attack Kleist feared then took place. The unfortunate Colonel Charles de Gaulle, long an advocate of specialised armoured warfare, was given command of a partially formed 4th Armoured Division with which, woefully under-manned and pitifully equipped though it was, he hit the Germans at Montcornet on that same 17 May. He lost some 35 of his precious tanks and shot up some of Guderian's transport, but the fact that the Panzers rolled forward once more speaks for itself.

The British commander, General Lord Gort, had come to the conclusion that he had to fall back to the coast with eventual evacuation as a possibility. In order to secure his southern flank he wanted to hold Arras, and the defenders of the town, Petreforce, under Major-general R. L. Petre, needed help. He therefore set up Frankforce, under Major-general Harold Franklyn, 'to support the garrison in Arras and to block the roads south of Arras, thus cutting off the German communications from the east... [and] occupy the line of the Scarpe on the east of Arras' and to make contact with the French on their left. General Billotte, when appraised of this plan, agreed that the French would attack at the same time with two divisions towards Cambrai. In the event this additional attack did not take place in concert with Frankforce's strike west of Arras, but was made on the following day.

On the afternoon of Tuesday 21 May two columns under the command of Major-general G. le Q. Martel moved south from the Vimy area. The two tank battalions and three battalions of Durham Light Infantry, together with four Royal Artillery batteries and a motor-cycle reconnaissance battalion of Northumberland Fusilers, made up the two columns of the advance. They ran into Rommel's 7th Panzer which had the SS-Division Totenkopf on its left and 5th Panzer on its right. Rommel had to intervene personally to steady his men and help throw the British back. By nightfall the British were obliged to withdraw, leaving Arras without the planned support and having suffered serious losses. This is what is often called the British counter-attack at Arras. The Germans were shaken by the experience. In his report Rommel declared that he had been hit by no fewer than five divisions. Nervousness was reinforced by the French foray towards Cambrai the next day.

On the northern front in Belgium Army Group B had been making steady but painful progress. The Belgians, to the surprise of the invaders, still resisted and the British alongside were falling back in good order. From the south Guderian had turned north and was fighting for Boulogne. The Guards had left the port for England on the evening of Thursday 23 May, but the French were still holding on and would continue to do so until Saturday. At Calais 1st Panzer had arrived on Thursday and would be relieved by 10th Panzer in due course, but the town would hold until the early hours of Monday.

The situation was therefore, as far as the Germans could see, that the allies were caught in the embrace of two army groups. They held two ports, just, on the west and then all the coast from Gravelines to the Wester Schelde, the waterway serving Antwerp. They thus had control of the ports of Zeebrugge, Ostend and Dunkirk as well as a hold in the west, however secure, on Calais and Boulogne. It may well be that the British planned an evacuation through Ostend which had excellent facilities. Bruges was still in Belgian hands, but the line was being pushed in towards Ypres in order to drive a wedge

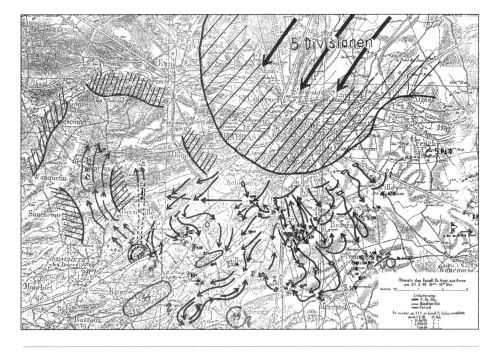

Rommel's version of the battle at Arras. He shows five divisions acting against him; a considerable exaggeration. (Holmes, Army Battlefield Guide, HMSO, 1995)

Three tanks lost in the mud near Veldhoek in the Ypres Salient, September 1917. (TM 1577/B3)

between the Belgians and the British. How long the Belgians could keep going was uncertain, but probably not for long, it was surprising that they had lasted until then. South of Ypres, including Lille and an equal distance beyond, the French First Army held a salient while, running northwest, the British and elements of the French had a line along the La Bassée Canal, properly called the Canal d'Aire. Somewhere there was the considerable remnants of Rommel's five divisions. It appeared that a German victory was assured but that the Allies still had considerable strength to strike back.

THE TERRAIN

The published data on the lands marked out for invasion was substantial. Complaints are heard of lack of maps, but they refer to maps of such scales as 1:25,000 – maps that can be used to appreciate terrain over which a battalion might attack. On the broader front the macro-data was good. On 29 February 1940 the Generalstab des Heeres Abteilung für Kriegskarten und Vermessungswesen, the army war map organisation in Berlin, published a massive information package for the forthcoming invasion. It included a geological map of Flanders, Artois and the lands north of the Somme. This was accompanied by booklets, one giving landscape photographs of the relevant countryside and another had detailed essays on the nature of the soils and rocks. This last drew on the work of such scholars as the British L.

Dudley Stamp and the American D. W. Johnson who had done detailed work on this area in the 1920s. For example, the diagram of the dugout (which may be seen in Peter Doyle's book, page 24) that appears on page 14 of the German handbook of 1940 is clearly based on the work of Alfred H. Brooks, published by the US Geological Survey in 1920. This was a work of scholarship and evidently for commanders miles away from the front, this was essential reference material.

A key to the map gives comments on the land, the 'various surfaces', under a number of headings of relevance to military decisions. These are: predominant soil types, rock strata and water content; predominant terrain forms, ground cover and land use; passability both by traffic and on foot over open terrain and temporary tracks or roads; obstacles and road block possibilities; permanent fortification and field defence suitability; artillery considerations; airforce considerations; drinking water supply; building material and aggregate extraction. Each of these topics receives specific comment, and the handbook offers broad commentary.

Of the terrain the Germans now faced and the Allies held, the coastal plain and dune belt, the handbook says:

In wet weather wide areas become boggy and impassable on foot. Vehicles can, in general, only move on the roads available which are very numerous and mostly fortified. These and the little railways run throughout on dykes; these form, with the numerous, in general not very wide, waterways, canals and ditches, a dense mesh of sections suitable for delaying defence.

At a breach or conscious destruction of the dykes, especially at high or spring tides, it will flood to a depth of 1.5 metres [5 feet] and be impassable, even if, according to the map, the height is between 1 and 3 metres. When the ebb tide takes the water away, there remains marsh.

Flooded fields and horse-drawn transport, a German soldier's photograph of 1940. (TM 5787/A3)

Drainage results through the collecting canals, from which the water reaches the sea through the great sluices of Calais, Gravelines and Dunkirk.

This does not sound like tank country.

The chalk uplands over which the Panzers had advanced are indicated in green on the geological map published in Berlin that February. Guines, due south of Calais, sits on the edge of the chalk, overlooking the area not merely marked with purple, but hatched to show that it lies below sea level. The surface is described as 'peat, with groundwater near the surface'. Guderian's 1st Panzer had already ventured into this area without serious mishap and was facing

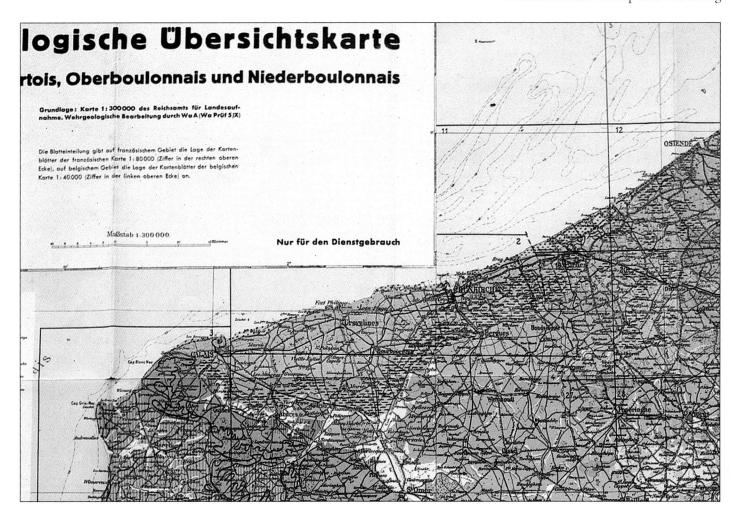

The German army geological map published in Berlin 29 February 1940. The description of terrain around Dunkirk given in the text (pages 5-6) applies to the purple area. The blue areas inland of that are similar to the terrain north-east of Ypres in front of the ridge crowned by Passchendaele. A firm ridge runs from the Guines, just south of Calais, through Ardres, branching south-east towards St Omer and north-east through Watten toward Bergues. (MME WW2 Maps MF3/5)

Gravelines. Here the purple lacks the hatching and the description is that much more encouraging. The surface is said to be of silt and clay, and in wet weather, while the soil is glutinous mud, the metalled roads are passable both by vehicles and on foot, although reconnaissance of all roads is necessary. The dense network of canals, however, does not prevent the whole area turning into marsh when wet, leaving only dyke-top roads for movement of any kind.

The line along which the Germans then stood runs southeast from Gravelines, following the white area on the map along the canalised River Aa to Watten and on by St Omer, Aire, and Béthune to La Bassée. Beyond, and inland of the purple area inside the yellow of the dunes, is a great blue area at this stage occupied by the Allies. It is bounded on the east by a crescent of dark yellow, showing a line of low hills known to veterans of the First World War as the Passchendaele Ridge. This blue surface is described by geologists as Ypres Clay. Infantry and tankmen of the previous war used more colourful terms. In dry weather, such as prevailed during the attack on the Messines Ridge in June 1917, the going was good. In wet weather, such as encountered during the Third Battle of Ypres or Passchendaele as it is also known, from 31 July 1917 until November that year, the conditions for fighting were intolerable. The Ypres Clay is impermeable, so water does not sink in but tries to flow off. Traffic and shellfire create mud, shellholes make muddy ponds and the terrain is soon reduced to a quagmire in which vehicles cannot move and men can even drown.

The River Aa at Watten, very credibly proposed as a line to be defended by Army Group A acting as anvil to the hammer of Army Group B. (MME WW2/3/24).

THE DECISION TO HALT

On Thursday morning, 23 May, German commanders were contemplating the High Command's orders for Army Group B to maintain its attacks on a broad front while Army Group A put in a thrust towards Dunkirk and Ypres. Kleist protested that half his tanks were now out of action and he was expected to guard the Somme front, deal with the Channel ports and now to launch a renewed attack eastwards; it was too much. On the same day OKH (Army High Command) decided to transfer the 4th Army, which included XV Panzer Corps with 5th and 7th Panzer, to the command of Army Group B. While all this was going on in the army, Göring was telephoning Hitler to propose that the Luftwaffe should be tasked with the destruction of the British Army, leaving the German Army merely to occupy the vacant ground.

Rundstedt's Army Group A was spread all across the landscape. The mechanised units had rushed on at a pace that had broken the Allies in two, but the bulk of the army was still using horse-drawn transport and foot-slogging it to catch up. The replacement of

Kleist's force on the Somme with infantry was delayed by this, as was the consolidation of the southeastern flank of the French-held salient based on Lille. The scatter shows clearly on the situation map for 25 May. While Army Group B has a tight wedge of divisions threatening the junction of the British and Belgian armies, Army Group A is all over the place, and it was now proposed to send the Panzers into the flatlands with little support. What was more, Kleist reported that, for the first time, the RAF had air superiority. Not only was it possible to fly out of English airfields, but, unknown to the Germans, British radar cover included the Pas de Calais.

On Friday 24 May, at 11.30am, Hitler arrived at Rundstedt's headquarters, now in Charleville-Mézières. Rundstedt put it to him that his army should stand firm while the infantry made the pace east of Arras. He also informed Hitler of the switch of the 4th Army to the northern command. Hitler approved the former and over-ruled the latter. At 12.31pm the Halt Order was issued. Colonel-general Halder, Chief of Staff at OKH, was compelled to recast his instructions, but attempted to preserve

part of his plan by issuing a permissive instruction allowing advances up to a line Dunkirk, Cassel, Estaires, Armentières, Ypres, Ostend. It was welcomed by Army Group B, but, because the manner of carrying out orders was their business, Army Group A did not relay the message to the front.

The factors that did not, according to the sources available, get discussed at all were the terrain and the weather. As far as the terrain was concerned, what was there to discuss? For everyone not actually on the ground the danger was clear. At the first drop of rain all movement would be confined to made-up roads and if put to it the allies would doubtless open the sluices just as the Belgians did in 1914. So even if the current fine weather held, water was still available.

To the immediate situation they faced must be added the requirement of taking the step after the next. The next step was, one way or another, the reduction of the allied salient. The one beyond that was the conquest of the rest of France, a vast country still in possession of substantial forces and for the defeat of which the Panzers were vital. There were no reserves, these Panzers were it. And, according to Kleist, half of them were out of action. So, the terrain was unsuitable for tanks, the infantry of Army Group B were thronging the eastern side of the salient, the Luftwaffe had made mincemeat of Warsaw and Rotterdam and are ready to do the same to the Channel ports and the Panzers had to be conserved. Four good reasons for the Halt Order.

THE REACTION

Guderian writes that he and his fellows were 'utterly speechless'. He recollects that the order said that Dunkirk, and Calais too if it proved difficult to take, should be left to the Luftwaffe. In admitting he quotes from memory he gives himself an excuse for inaccuracy. The halt order actually made it clear that Guderian was to create a line against which the allies could be crushed. Instead he continued his policy of creeping forward when forbidden to move at all.

South of the La Bassée Canal Rommel was in cheerful form. On 24 May he wrote to his wife to say that all was going well and that if anything the weather was not merely lovely but that there was too much sun.
On Sunday 26 May he wrote again, saying,

A day or two without action has done a lot of good. The division has lost up to date 27 officers killed and 33 wounded, and 1,500 men dead and wounded. That's about 12 per cent casualties. Very little compared with what's been achieved … Food, drink and sleep are all back to routine.

On 25 May Field Marshal Walther von Brauchitsch, the German commander-in-chief, implored Hitler to permit Army Group A to advance, but was refused. Halder noted in his diary,

… our political leadership feels that the decisive battle must be fought not in Flanders, but in northern France. But in order to camouflage this political objective, we are told that the terrain in Flanders, with its many waterways, is not suitable for armoured operations … Another thing, the Luftwaffe, on which so much hope is now being placed, is completely dependent on the weather

Halder fails to point out that, in the terrain into which he wishes to send the tanks, the weather is also crucial for the Panzers. Nor does he mention the intensity of the Lutfwaffe attacks on the Channel ports that day.

On Sunday 26 May the situation appeared to be static, with the French southeast of Lille not merely resisting, but undertaking counter-attacks and

Sepp Dietrich crossed the Aa, contrary to orders, and took position on the hill above Watten, part of the ridge embracing the terrain south and west of the Dunkirk enclave. (MME WW2/3/26).

the Belgians standing firm, save for a crack in the line at Courtrai, while signal traffic suggested a build-up of allied forces south of the Somme. At 3.30pm the order to move once more was given. Calais fell later that day and Guderian's force attempted to move forward that night and made some progress on the Monday. The essential change came on the Ypres front where the Germans broke through at Zonnebeke and the King of the Belgians signalled Gort to warn that they could hold out very little longer. The message failed to arrive and it was nearly midnight, surrender hour for the Belgians, before Gort was aware of the collapse of the northern front. No alternative to evacuation now existed for the allies.

Now, at last, it rained. As the British and French fell back, fighting as they went, the task became one of keeping the sides of the bag in place to allow troops to pull back towards the canal between Bergues and Furnes, a postion flanked with friendly marsh. Rommel, once across the La Bassée canal on Tuesday 28 May, moved northeast to Lomme, just outside Lille, to shut off the French there. Guderian's Panzer Corps was being relieved by the XIV Motorised Corps on Wednesday 29 May, the day 1st Panzer took Gravelines.

Guderian felt the matter had been mishandled. He wrote:

The operation would have been completed very much more quickly if Supreme Headquarters had not kept ordering XIX Army Corps [Panzer Corps] to stop and thus hindered its rapid and successful advance. What the future course of the war would have been if we had succeeded at that time in taking the British Expeditionary Force prisoner at Dunkirk, it is now impossible to guess … Unfortunately the opportunity was wasted owing to Hitler's nervousness. The reason he subsequently gave for holding back my

The Canal d'Aire, also known as the La Bassee Canal, at Gorre where the 1st Royal Irish Fusiliers faced Rommel's 7th Panzer Division. (MME WW2/4/7).

Renault R35 of 1st Tank Regiment. (© Osprey Publishing Ltd., from Campaign 3: France 1940 by Alan Shepperd, Illustration by Terry Hadler)

PzKpfw II Ausf. B of 7th Panzer Regiment, 10 Panzer Division. (© Osprey Publishing Ltd., from Campaign 3: France 1940 by Alan Shepperd, Illustration by Terry Hadler)

The German Decision-makers

The Halt Order was given by a man, or men, some 140 miles (225km) away from the front, acting on an appreciation of incoming information with reference to already available data and informed by training and experience.

At the front was **Heinz Guderian**, an officer who had come from a relatively humble background and had served as a signals officer early in the First World War, rising to a Staff post, but with little front-line experience. After that war he became involved in matters of transport, serving on the staff of General E. Tschischwitz, head of Motor Transport Troops. Here he developed his ideas of combined operations, bringing together tanks, artillery, engineers and mobile infantry, that were to be the foundations of German success in 1939 and 1940. His book, *Achtung – Panzer!* was published in 1937 in German and did not appear in English until 1992. In it he set out his three essentials for success in tank warfare – surprise, deployment en masse and suitable terrain. He said:

As for terrain, the tank forces should be committed only where there are no obstacles that exceed the capacity of their machines; otherwise the armoured attack will break on the terrain ... Tanks have a certain capacity, just like men and animals; when one's demands exceed that capacity, they will fail. Since we cannot hope to find favourable terrain for tanks everywhere, we must strive to employ them where they can move and show their striking power to the best advantage.

He continues to repeat his belief in the value the role of tactical aircraft working together with tanks. While one cannot propose that his superiors were re-reading his text each night before they slept, it is not too much to think that the three basic rules – surprise, numbers, terrain – remained part of their mental landscape.

Colonel-general Rudolf Gerd von Runstedt had come out of retirement to command Army Group South in the Polish campaign of 1939. He had served in the 22nd Reserve Division in 1914 and claimed to have been with sight of the Eiffel Tower but experienced the bitterness of having victory snatched away by the flair with which the French counter-attacked. He was then posted to the Eastern Front where the war remained much more open and mobile than in the west. The perils of Flanders were thus known to him at second hand, but the dangers of exposed flanks was something he had dealt with in person. Now some 65 years old, he was open to new concepts but inclined to caution; the French seemed able to pull something extra out of the bag just when you thought you had them beaten. That Runstedt reported to OKH, the German Army Headquarters, would worry **Adolf Hitler** not at all. He was quite ready to by-pass normal channels of communication and speak direct to the commander in the field. Hitler himself had served in the First World War in the 16th Bavarian Infantry. He was in the Ypres sector in 1914 where he won the Iron Cross (Second Class) for rescuing an officer under fire and he was there again in 1917, at the Third Battle of Ypres which floundered in a sea of mud. He had been gassed in 1916 and in 1918 was awarded his second Iron Cross, this time First Class. Although he attained only the rank of corporal, his front line experience was considerable. The sight of the primitive tanks of the First World War bogged down in the Ypres mud cannot but have remained vivid in his mind.

corps – that the ground in Flanders with its many ditches and canals was not suited to tanks – was a poor one.

And there the argument is usually left to rest, with Hitler responsible for irrational fears and Guderian the hero of the new warfare. The war diary of the Kleist Group records that Guderian made an inspection of the ground that day, Wednesday 29 May, and reported to the Chief of Staff as follows:

(1) After the Belgian capitulation continuation of operations here is not desirable as it is costing unnecessary sacrifices. The armoured divisions have only 50 per cent of their armoured strength left ...

(2) A tank attack is pointless in the marshy country which has been completely soaked by rain. The troops are in possession of the high ground south of Dunkirk; they hold the important Cassel-Dunkirk road; and they have favourable artillery positions ...

Furthermore 18 Army [of Army Group B] is approaching ... from the east. The infantry forces of this army are more suitable than tanks for fighting in this kind of country, and the task of closing the gap on the coast can therefore be left to them.

The echoes of the verdict of the geological handbook and map are striking. Irrational and loathsome though Hitler was in many instances, here he was exercising a prudent caution. The Halt Order was based on a number of factors and was a logical outcome of considering them. There had been attacks by the allies on the Panzers which Guderian minimised and Rommel exaggerated, each for his own purposes. The speed of the advance had left the Germans thin on the ground. Above all, there was just what Guderian had warned against, terrain on which an armoured attack would break, terrain beyond their capacity – when it rained. And it did. If the tanks had gone in, they would not have come out, and if they had not come out General Weygand's line north of Paris might have held. If the Halt Order contributed to the losing of the war in the long term, it also made it possible to win in the short term.

ACKNOWLEDGEMENTS
The author would like to thank Professor Peter Doyle of the University of Greenwich for his helpful comments which have prevented at least some of the errors that would otherwise mar the geological information, and Nigel Read for translation of the German military maps and manual. All errors are, of course, those of the author alone.

REFERENCES
Anon., *Militärgeographische Beschreibung von Frankreich, Teil I, Nordost-Frankreich*, (Berlin, 1940)

Benoist-Méchin, J., trans. Peter Wiles, *Sixty Days that Shook the West*, (London, 1963)

Colville, J. R., *Man of Valour: The Life of Field Marshal the Viscount Gort*, (London, 1972)

Doyle, Peter, *Geology of the Western Front, 1914-1918*, (London, 1998)

Ellis, L. F., *The War in France and Flanders 1939-1940*, (London, 1954)

Guderian, Heinz, *Achtung - Panzer!*, trans. Christopher Duffy, (London, 1992)

Guderian, Heinz, *Panzer Leader*, trans. Constantine Fitzgibbon, (London, 1952)

Horne, Alistair, *To Lose a Battle: France 1940*, (London, 1969)

Rommel, Erwin, ed. B.H. Liddell Hart, *The Rommel Papers*, (London, 1953)

Snyder, Louis L., *Encyclopedia of the Third Reich*, (London, 1998)

Jacobsen, H.-A. and J. Rohwer, eds., trans. Edward Fitzgerald, *Decisive Battles of World War II: the German View*, (London, 1965)

Wehrgeologische Übersichtskarte von Flandern, *Artois, Oberboulonnais und Niederboulonnais*, (Berlin, 1940)

ABOUT THE AUTHOR

Martin Marix Evans is the author of a number of books for Osprey, including *Passchendaele and the Battles of Ypres 1914-1918*, *Retreat Hell! We Just got Here! – The American Expeditionary Force in France 1917-1918* and *The Boer War – South Africa 1899-1902*. Martin has just finished *The Fall of France – Act with Daring*, due for publication in May 2000 **(see Messenger pages for ordering details plus World War II books special offers)**.

Last Days: after the Halt Order was lifted, Lille was cut off by 7th Panzer and the Dunkirk enclave took on its final form. (© Osprey Publishing Limited)

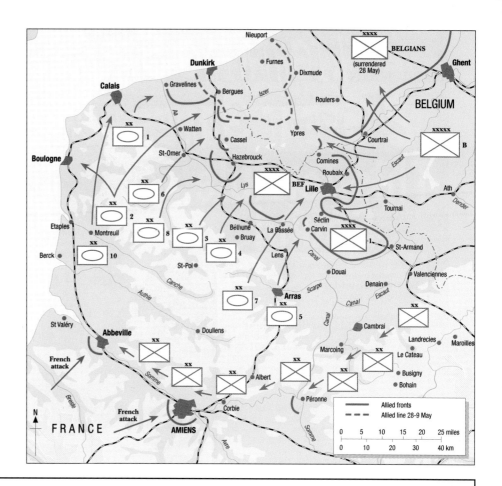

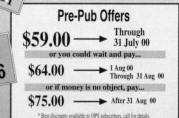
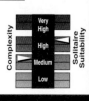

'A New Method of Attack'

The German assault on Eben-Emael, 10 May 1940

MAJOR T N MOUAT MBE RLC

'... did our high-tech equipment really work? Beyond our wildest expectations'
General Norman Schwarzkopf, *It Doesn't Take a Hero* (Bantam, 1992)

German soldiers carrying 50 kg hollow charges at Fort Aubin-Neufchâteau (Coll. Franck Vernier).

On 10 May 1940, German forces attacked into Belgium and Holland. Blocking their way was the Belgian fort of Eben Emael, accepted as one of the most powerful single fortifications in Europe with a garrison of 1,200 men. It was rendered inoperative in less than two hours by a German force of only 56 men armed with man-portable weapons.

HOW WAS THIS ACHIEVED?

The accepted wisdom at the time, and still prevalent, is that the element of surprise gained by the use of gliders, and the use of emerging technology, in the shape of the 'hollow–charge', were the reasons for success. The Commander of this 'Lilliputian detachment', Lieutenant Rudolf Witzig, supported this view in his own account of the raid.

In March 1991, I was taking a party of soldiers in a guided tour over the Belgian fort of Eben Emael, with the help of the Belgian 'Friends of Eben Emael' (FEE) an association of veterans and local historians. At one point during the tour on the outside of the fort, the party was grouped around one of the steel cupolas that formed the basis of the fort's armament. Standing on the cupola, to address the group more easily, I gave a short explanation on the theory of the 'hollow charges' used by the Germans in their attack, and pointed to the characteristic marks left on the armour plate from their operation. One of the soldiers then asked what sort of effect the charge had on the men working inside. I indicated the veteran standing to one side, and said 'Why don't you ask him? He was inside one of these turrets during the attack.' The soldier did so; but the veteran merely shrugged expansively and said 'I suppose it made me more religious ...' He then pointed out that the 'hollow charge' had not in fact knocked out the turret, but merely temporarily jammed the traversing mechanism. The knockout blow came from a number of smaller conventional charges 'thrown down the barrels of the guns'.

This account was a surprise and appeared to be quite opposite to the accepted view. It was not, however, the first time that it has come to light.

It has been mentioned, and dismissed as apocryphal, in other accounts of the attack on the Fort. But if this veteran's account did turn out to be true, it raises a number of interesting questions. Why has there been this tendency to exaggerate the value of technology? If it was not the use of some 'secret weapon' that contributed most to the defeat of the Fort in 1940, then was it something else?

PLANNING AND TRAINING

In 1939 the German Army Group B was given the task of planning the breakthrough of the Belgian defences between Venlo and Aachen in a lightning operation, and destroying the Belgian forces before they could occupy the defensive line constructed across the centre of Belgium.

When the Army Commander, General von Reichenau presented his operational plan to Hitler and the Supreme Army Command (OKH), in October 1939, the Fuhrer was not satisfied with the idea of taking the bridges over the Meuse and Albert Canal by the advance guard of the 6th Army. He was concerned that the defenders would have enough time to blow the bridges. This would slow down the mechanised units, allowing the Belgians time to withdraw as they had in 1914 and extend the enemy front as far as the coast. The whole operational concept hinged on the destruction of Fort Eben Emael and the capture of the Albert Canal bridges, at the very beginning of the campaign.

On 27 October 1939, General Kurt Student, Commander of 7 Fliger Division was ordered to visit the Fuhrer, 'alone and without delay'. On arrival, the thoroughly puzzled General was immediately led in to see Hitler. At the far end of the long walnut panelled room, the Fuhrer raised his eyes and beckoned the General to look at the map on his desk. 'For the war in the West ...' Hitler paused, seeming to consider how to begin, '... I know you have made some tests with gliders. You have some in your Division. I have a job for you and I want to know if you can do it. The Belgians have a fort here ... The top is like a grassy meadow. They have heavy artillery in cupolas and casemates. I think some of our silent gliders could land on top of the fort and your men storm the works. Is that possible?'

To Student the idea sounded both incredible and simple. He said that he was not sure and would have to go away and think about it. He returned the next day, still not sure. He said to Hitler, 'It may be possible under very special circumstances: the landing must

The 120mm gun turret in the centre of Eben Emael, the scar of a hollow charge can just be seen. (Bernard Vrijens)

be made in daylight, or at least morning twilight and not before; and I am uncertain about the amount and type of explosives needed to be used against the fortifications.'

Hitler then revealed that German munitions experts had developed a new and fantastic explosive charge, the *Hohlladung* or 'Hollow Charge'. It was capable of blowing a hole in any known military armament, be it steel or concrete. The problem was that it weighed 50kg and could not be fired from a gun, but had to be emplaced, fused and exploded, by two or three men. If it could be placed like this, nothing could withstand it.

Student had been considering how a few glider loads of men could really capture such a vast fortification with conventional explosives. With the hollow charge the whole operation took on a new meaning and chance of success. The combination of gliders and hollow charges seemed unbeatable to him. Hitler then said 'I order you to take Fort Eben-Emael. All aspects of the operation must remain absolutely secret. The code name for this operation will be GRANIT' (Granite). Later Student was to say that this 'was perhaps the most original idea of this rich-in-brain-waves man'.

Now that the decision had been made, the preparations for the attack went ahead. General Student carefully screened his airborne forces and selected Hauptmann S. A. Koch, a highly talented officer, renowned for his incredible ideas and schemes, to lead the attack. On 3 November 1939, Koch Storm Detachment was formed in Hildesheim, composed of a number of units. These were formed into groups, including GRANIT who consisted of 11 gliders, two Officers and 88 men.

The GRANIT force was formed from the Engineer Detachment of the Division, under the command of Lt. Witzig. This was the only parachute

A DFS 230 attack glider. This particular glider was captured by the British in North Africa.

unit composed entirely of sappers. Many of these had long records of disciplinary infractions, but they were all individualists with a reputation for fearlessness. Amongst them were some of the best pre-war amateur glider pilots.

This detachment was constantly moved around under a bewildering array of codenames. Glider practice in the Hildesheim area was carried out on only the smallest scale. When necessary, the gliders were dismantled and moved about in furniture vans. Despite their extensive sport experience, most of the pilots had never seen the DFS 230 before, and they entered into an intensive training programme. By March 1940 they could take off at night, towed by a JU-52 aircraft, and cast off to land within 20m of the target. They used a piece of terrain in Stolberg that was similar to the plateau at Eben-Emael.

Each section, one glider, was given two emplacements to destroy, with plans to take over another section's task, should it fail to arrive. The glider pilots were also fully integrated into the sections. Practice assaults and trial demolitions were carried out on Polish fortifications near Gleiwitz. Secrecy was of paramount importance. From

November 1939 until May 1940, for six months, the men of the operation were virtual prisoners. No mail, no leave, no contact with other units and all parachute insignia was removed from their uniforms. Two men, found discussing the operation with men of another unit, were sentenced to be shot, but were reprieved to take part on the day of the operation. Eventually, trains moved the planes by night to two airfields near Cologne. The hangars were continuously guarded and surrounded by barbed wire. Even the base commanders were not told what was going on in the hangars.

The operation was scheduled to start at 0300hrs on 10 May 1940. Two Luftwaffe personnel who were curious, and were found wandering in the vicinity of the hangars the evening before, were arrested and held until the operation was over. By 0335hrs on 10 May 1940 all of Witzig's gliders had taken off and their tow planes circled to gain height before following the route marked by searchlights and signal beacons.

THE FORT

Before World War I, the Belgian fort designer Henri Alexis Brialmont had

From Eben-Emael above the Albert Canal, the Maas is overlooked to the south-east. (B751/96/27A)

identified the 'Gap of Vise' as being of vital strategic importance, and stated that the decision not to construct a fort in this locality was one over which the Belgian nation would 'weep tears of blood'. The events of 1914 proved him right. Later, during the construction of the Albert Canal (1927-29) a cutting was driven through a hill in the area, known as the Kaster, over 80 metres deep. This feat of engineering, equal in magnitude to the cuts at Suez and Panama, was to connect the canal to the Meuse River. This produced a site with the near-vertical walls of the cutting to the northeast, a natural cliff to the south and unparalleled views towards Germany. With the lesson of the First World War behind them, and the engineering works producing near-ideal conditions, the Belgians decided to construct a fortification near the village of Eben Emael. The Fort was constructed in only three years (between 1932 and 1935) at a cost of Bf 24M (1935 prices), and occupied an area of 75 hectares.

The armament consisted of two batteries, one for protection of the fort itself, and the other designed to cover the vital bridges over the Meuse and Albert Canal. The latter was made up of a number of cupolas and casemates. The three cupolas had all-round traverse. Two of them were of the 'disappearing' variety, capable of being completely retracted between firings. In addition to these real cupolas, three fake cupolas (identical to the largest) were added as a deception plan to confuse attackers. The four casemates each consisted of three-gun batteries with a limited arc designed to cover specific bridges. The defensive battery included anti-aircraft positions and machine-gun emplacements on the roof of the fort, as well as a defensive ring of blockhouses and outworks.

The fort itself benefited from the latest technology. It possessed a sophisticated fire-control system and network of outlying observer stations to co-ordinate defensive fire tasks. The chemical threat was addressed with a

protection system of unparalleled ingenuity, involving purified air overpressure maintained in the gun positions and a huge filtration chamber. Gas-tight doors separated the various parts of the fort and each section had, in theory, three separate modes of communication with the command post. The fort was supported by six massive generators and even had its own deep borehole well.

THE ASSAULT

As dawn was breaking on 10 May, the German gliders landed on the surface of the fort. Despite the months of planning and training, there were a number of potentially fatal mishaps. One of the gliders was damaged at the take-off and another, carrying Witzig who was commanding the operation, was forced to land near Cologne due to the towing cable breaking. The wind changed; the gliders could not be released until they had passed into Dutch airspace, where they were detected and fired on by the anti-aircraft batteries around Maastricht. This alerted the Belgian defenders, who were already at their posts after an alert had been called at 0030hrs. In addition the Belgian deception plan worked perfectly and the Germans wasted 30 per cent of their force attacking the dummy cupolas.

The Belgians, however, had problems of their own. The fort itself was regarded as something of a punishment posting, and was not popular. The full garrison was indeed 1,200 men. However, this was made up of about 200 technicians and support staff and 1,000 gunners. These were split into two week-long shifts, with the off-duty shift billeted at Wonck. They had no transport and it usually took over an hour to march the 6km to the fort, and in the past few months of the 'Phoney War' a great many alerts had been called, all of which turned out to false alarms - until now. The total of

500 gunners actually in the fort was further depleted by sickness (the fort was not a particularly healthy place to work) and the policy of allowing fathers with large families, and those from agricultural areas, extra time off at home. In fact, on 10 May 1940 the total garrison was only 883. Furthermore, much of the administration for the garrison was carried out from two wooden huts situated outside the main entrance. In the event of an attack, classified documents and other materials had to be moved into the fort's command post. The men allocated to this task were the crews of the machine gun emplacements on the upper level of the fort. Despite this, the commander of the fort, Major Jean Jottrand acted swiftly. When he heard the sound of the anti-aircraft batteries firing he ordered the transfer of papers and the demolition of the huts that limited the arcs of fire for the outer blockhouses. When the demolition guard at the nearby bridge at Kanne contacted him, because they were unable to contact their superiors, Jottrand ordered them to open fire even though this was exceeding his orders. Despite not being under his command, they obeyed him and eventually destroyed the bridge in the face of the attacking German ground forces. Jottrand did organise a number of counter-attacks, but these were ineffectual. The soldiers moving the documents into the fort were the crew on the machine-gun emplacements on the roof, so were absent from their posts for the vital moments that they were needed. The Fort commander did not have formal communication links with the surrounding ground units and, anyway, they were not under his command. Any requests for assistance were supposed to be relayed through the superior headquarters at Liege. The off-duty shift at Wonck was contacted and ordered to attack, but the Germans

on the Fort called down Stuka and artillery attacks and the attack petered out. Only 12 men reached the fort 'unwounded and capable of mounting an attack'. They were used in counter-attacks, but after running out of their stock of grenades Jottrand called them back.

WHAT ABOUT THE HOLLOW CHARGES?

While all this was going on, however, it is generally accepted that the German hollow charges were making

short work of the Belgian guns and emplacements. But was this really the case? I am an Ammunition Technical Officer (ATO) by training, and not unfamiliar with the effects of explosives. I examined the other turrets and casemates during this visit, and later. In only one case, out of a total of 14 gun positions, was it possible that the hollow charges achieved the destruction of the gun concerned. In all other cases the demolition was achieved either by a smaller conventional charge. These

Oberleutnant, Jäger and NCO, shown in typical uniform and equipment for the fighting in Western Europe 1940. (Artwork by Mike Chappell from Men-at-Arms 139 German Airborne Troops, © Osprey Publishing Limited).

were placed near the barrels of the guns themselves, or by wedging the hollow charge at an angle in the embrasure and relying on the force of the explosion rather than the hollow charge effect to destroy the gun. The charges only appear to have been truly effective in shattering the tiny observation cupolas that were mounted on the top of some of the emplacements.

In the days after the attack, the alarmist contemporary accounts of German secret weapons, spies, and sabotage were easy to understand. One newspaper even offered the fantastic theory that Germans, living in that part of Belgium, had managed to stack explosives in caves under the Fort so they only needed to detonate them when the attack started. Later speculation focused on the Belgian consortium, United Enterprises, which received the contract to build the Fort. They sub-contracted some of the work to German firms. Not surprisingly, this led to much speculation about espionage, despite the fact that their work was limited to the canal walls. In any case the Belgian Government, of course, made details of the armament of the Fort, as well as its level of protection public. How else were they to provide a deterrent to any potential attacker?

In the final analysis, the fort itself was the embodiment of the latest military defensive technology and the only readily acceptable explanation for its defeat was the invention of some more advanced technology that made resistance impossible. Furthermore, the comprehensive German security precautions and unusual treatment of the Fort's garrison after the attack (they were completely isolated in a separate prison camp for six months) did nothing to dispel the rumours and mythology that built up.

But, if it was not the advantage of technology that proved the deciding factor, what did?

On 10 May 1940, the German Paratroopers of Assault Force GRANIT were some of the finest soldiers in the world. They had a great many advantages on their side: the rigorous physical selection, the months of practice attacks and training carried out in the strictest secrecy, and the long record of fighting and other disciplinary infractions that is supposed to demonstrate aggressiveness and high morale in a unit. There were additional factors. The German soldiers believed themselves to be superior to their enemy. The invasion of Poland had been a stunning success, the latest in a line of German political and military triumphs. The enemy were 40 year-old conscripts, wearing uniforms little changed from the last time the German Army had defeated them. They were armed with Belgian copies of German First World War rifles and had received minimal infantry training.

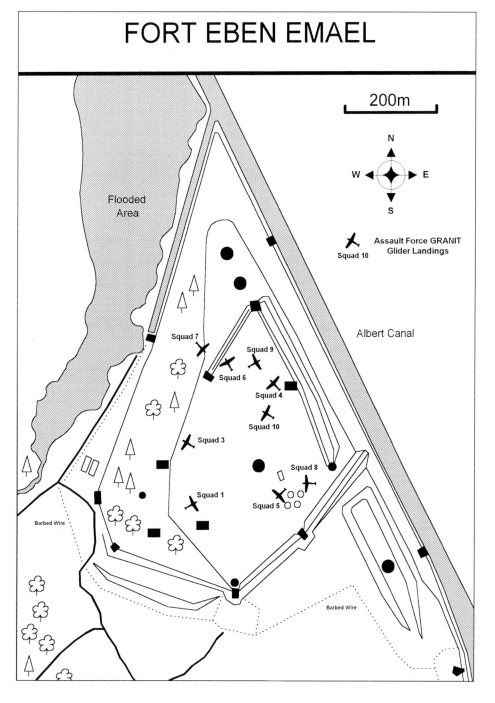

FORT EBEN EMAEL

The Belgian leadership lacked focus and direction. They were unprepared for war, both physically and morally.

LATECOMERS

When the tow cable snapped on his glider, forcing Lt. Witzig down, most normal men would have accepted that their part in the operation was over. Witzig, however, did not allow this setback to deter him. He hijacked a bicycle from a passing civilian and set off to his base. After meeting up with a German unit, he commandeered transport and drove to the airfield some 70km away.

There he picked up a spare cable, a set of wheels for the glider (these were jettisoned on take-off) and arranged for a new JU-52 tug aircraft from the airfield at Goetersich. He then took off and flew back and landed where his glider had been forced down, the JU-52 was capable of landing on unprepared fields. In the meantime his men had not been idle. They cut down the hedges dividing the fields, allowing room for the landing and take-off. When Witzig arrived they fitted the cable, lifted the glider onto the new wheels and took off again for the Fort. They finally arrived only two hours late. By then, however, it was all over.

Yet they were not content to rest on their laurels. They took on the Fort's garrison itself, 80 men against 800. They blasted their way into Maastricht 1 & 2, and MG Nord by wedging hollow charges at an angle in the embrasures of the guns. In Maastricht 1 the gun was thrown back off its mounting, and the surviving crew fled down to the safety of the interior of the Fort. The Germans then squeezed through the hole caused by the explosion and into the casemate. The dismounted gun had blocked the door to the telephone point, trapping two of the Belgian gun crew, and these were freed by the Germans. The attackers then decided to press on after the

A 60mm anti-tank gun, probably the best in the world in May 1940, at Fort Battice. (Coll. Franck Vernier)

retreating Belgians. The connection to the intermediate level of the Fort is via a steel spiral staircase that winds its way around the ammunition hoists, over a vertical distance of 40 metres. The Germans made their way down the stair to the intermediate level, and up to the blast doors.

These blast doors were heavy gas-tight double steel doors, 2 metres apart and closing towards each other. Between the locked doors were 20cm slots in the concrete, into which fitted a number of steel 'I' beams completely blocking the passage. Sandbags were available to fill up the remaining space between the beams and the second set of doors further backed these. Finally the doors themselves were capable of being locked. This formidable arrangement was supposed to defeat any attempts to get into the interior of the Fort.

German soldiers carried hollow charges all the way down the winding stairs, to the blast doors. It is worth remembering that the charge alone weighed 50kg, and the steel stairs are

too narrow to allow two fully equipped soldiers to pass each other. At the bottom they set the fuses and retreated to the surface. How long was that fuse? Lt. Witzig states that the standard fuses were only 10 seconds. The soldiers must have fitted non-standard fuses, something that is always to be avoided in the heat of battle, where a simple slip would cause instant disaster or embarrassing failure. Neither of these happened, and the resulting explosion, confined as it was deep underground, had only two routes for the expanding gases to escape; up the shaft containing the stair and ammunition hoists, and through the blast doors. Behind the doors in Maastricht 1 were six Belgian soldiers on guard. They were killed instantly as the door and the steel beams were blasted across the passage. Also in the corridor were a number of drums containing a chlorine-based disinfectant. These burst sending the smell of chlorine, via the forced air system, throughout the Fort. The concussion and the smell of gas caused a panic among the remaining defenders.

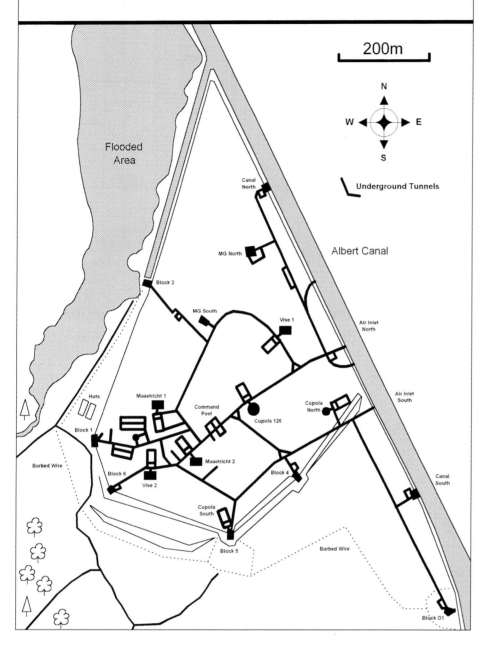

FORT EBEN EMAEL

200m

N
W E
S

Underground Tunnels

Flooded Area

Albert Canal

Canal North

MG North

Block 2

MG South

Vise 1

Air Inlet North

Huts

Maastricht 1

Command Post

Cupola North

Cupola 120

Air Inlet South

Block 1

Maastricht 2

Barbed Wire

Block 6

Vise 2

Block 4

Canal South

Cupola South

Block 5

Barbed Wire

Block O1

Unfortunately for the Germans, the force of the explosions also destroyed the steel stairs and ammunition hoists, leaving them an impassable mass of twisted metal, preventing access to the intermediate levels. Nevertheless they continued to attack the various embrasures until they ran out of explosives.

Even the crew of the glider that was damaged on take-off did not return to base, but instead commandeered various vehicles and joined the ground forces for the link-up attack. Some crossed the canal in advance of the attacking forces, over the wreckage of the demolished bridge at Kanne. One of them, Private Walter 'P' Meier, stole a bicycle and cycled right up to the fort, where his comrades who didn't recognise him promptly fired on him. He returned to German lines with a copy of the 'Orders for the Day', taken from a notice board outside the main

entrance, and 121 Belgian prisoners (the POW Camp receipt for the prisoners he attached to his battle report to prove he hadn't been slacking).

The Belgians, in contrast, limited themselves to ineffectual counter-attacks (despite outnumbering their foe by odds of 10:1) and calling down artillery fire onto the superstructure of the Fort.

CONCLUSIONS

Operation GRANIT was a plan based on the technological possibilities of the hollow charge. It was carried out with overwhelming success, despite the fact that this technology proved almost completely ineffectual, because of the fighting qualities of the German attackers, and the lack of those qualities in the Belgian defenders. Ultimately, the Germans were simply better soldiers than their foes.

But if this was the case, why did even veterans of the assault feel compelled to exaggerate the value of the technology, and why we are still doing so 50 years later?

I feel the answer lies in the fact that western society has a technological foundation. We are used to technology, and technical explanations are easy for us to understand. We find comfort in machines, lacking as they are supposed to be in 'human failings' and they give us confidence. Also, in the post-colonial era, there is a natural unwillingness for a westerner to compare himself with his enemy man to man, person to person. It smacks of arrogance, overconfidence and ultimately racism. It just isn't done.

Furthermore, the soldier is well aware that, although technology is only one factor in the reason for victory, it is a factor over which he has little control. It is within his power to change the emphasis on training, organisation and doctrine but it is the politician that will ultimately decide whether he receives the latest piece of equipment or not.

If this is true of the victors, then it is doubly so of the losers. It is only human nature to put the blame for failure on something over which you have no control. Thus we end up with both sides appearing to agree on the reason for success, when the reality was somewhat different.

In the end it is inevitable that technology will receive inflated importance. It is also only natural that accounts of the event will pay less emphasis on long and complicated explanations about morale, aggression, team spirit and esprit de corps, in favour of a sophisticated illustration showing the way a hollow charge is supposed to work. Technological factors can never be ignored, but Operation GRANIT offers a classic example of how their significance has been greatly exaggerated and served to obscure the real reasons for the success of the operation.

Which brings me back to the quote by Swarzkopf at the start of this article.

Did our high-tech equipment really work 'beyond our wildest expectations'?

BIBLIOGRAPHY

Griffith, Paddy: *Forward Into Battle*, (1981).

Grossman, Lt Col David A: *On Killing*, (Final working draft, not yet published), 1993.

Keegan, John: *The Face of Battle*, (Penguin 1978)

Lucas, James: *Kommando*, (Arms & Armour Press)

Mrazek, Lt Col James E: *The Fall of Eben Emael*, (Presidio, 1991)

Pimlott, John L (Ed): *The World At Arms*, (Reader's Digest Assn Ltd, 1989)

Regan, Geoffrey: *The Guinness Book Of Military Blunders*, (Guinness, 1991)

Schwarzkopf, Gen N: *It Doesn't Take A Hero*, (Bantam Press, 1992)

Vliegen, Rene: *Fort Eben-Emael*, FEE (1987)

Wood, Alan: *History Of The World's Glider Forces*, (Patrick Stephens Ltd, 1990)

ABOUT THE AUTHOR

Major Tom Mouat MBE is a serving officer in the British Army and a specialist in ammunition and explosives. This is first piece of work for Osprey.

EDITORIAL NOTE

The opinions expressed in this article are the author's own and in no way represent the views of Her Majesty's Government. For more details on this subject see *The Fall of France – Act with Daring* by Martin Marix Evans (Osprey) available May 2000 **(see Messenger pages for ordering details plus World War II books special offers)**.

Hohlladungen (Hollow-Charges)

The German hollow charges were quite different from the 'shaped charges' used today in anti-tank missiles and demolition charges. They were hemispherical 50kg charges, with a simple hemispherical cavity in the centre of the base.

At the time the physical principal was not clearly understood (nor, indeed, is it totally understood today). The effect was first discovered in America in 1888. Munroe noticed that the manufacturers details, engraved into the surface of a slab of explosive produced engraved reflections in the surface of the metal he was trying to blow up. He experimented with cutting cavities into explosive charges, and was amazed to find that these cavities produced cavities of their own in their target This became known as 'The Munroe Effect'. Modern charges make used of a liner inside the cavity of a dense and malleable material which is formed by the force of the explosion into a jet of material that blasts its way through the target. Gold would be particularly effective, but for obvious reasons copper is normally used. This jet takes some distance to form, so modern charges use a 'stand-off' distance to ensure the charge explodes at the optimum distance. As a rule of thumb, the best 'stand-off' distance is about 4 cone-diameters and the penetration through mild steel is about 6 cone diameters. The effect of this cavity liner was not fully understood in 1939, and it was not appreciated what a difference the angle and shape of the cavity, and choice of material of the liner, would make to the penetrating power. The 'Munroe Effect' charges were, however, far more effective than conventional explosives in attacking concrete, and armour plate when the thickness of the armour was less than the cavity size in the charge. In Eben Emael, however, the armour plate on the gun cupolas (but not the observation cupolas) had a greater thickness than the penetrating power. This meant that any damage behind the armour was only achieved by the shock wave producing 'spalling' (fragments of metal braking off the inside of the armour) in a way similar to that achieved by modern High Explosive Squash Head (HESH) shells. This only happens in certain types of steel armour, and very rarely through concrete.

A point of fascinating historical coincidence is that the Swiss engineer Morhaupt presented the Hollow Charge to the French Army equivalent of the Ordnance Board, who accepted it into service on 10 May 1940.

The heroes of the attack, decorated with the Knight's Cross by Adolf Hitler. From the left, Delica, Witzig, Koch, Zierach, Ringler, Meissner, Kiess, Altmann and Jäger. (B74/113/13)

Moor against Majus

The defence of Spain and Morocco against the Vikings 844–972AD

David Nicolle PhD

Animal head post ('The Academic') from the Oseberg Viking tomb, Norway. (Universitetets Oldsaksamling, Oslo)

For a period of just over 130 years two very different cultures, their geographical and ethnic origins far apart, clashed at the outer limits of their respective territories, the open sea and coastlines of the Iberian peninsular and North Africa their battleground. Most of the countries that felt the fury of the Northmen during the main period of Viking raiding had clearly been visited by Scandinavian merchants of an earlier generation, whether in Russia, Central or Western Europe, or the British Isles.

The Muslim territories of Andalus and Morocco are unlikely to have been different. Here the Scandinavians or Norsemen were generally known as Majus or 'Magi' because Arab explorers noted an apparent similarity between fire-worshipping aspects of Nordic paganism and the significance of fire to the Zoroastrians or Magi of Iran. Sometimes, however, the word Majus simply meant pagans, and so the exact identity of those Majus who helped King Alfonso II of Galicia against an Andalusian Islamic army in 795 AD remains unclear. Most scholars believe them to have been Basques, since paganism was still strong amongst these people, but the possibility that they were early Viking visitors cannot be entirely ruled out.

The Majus who attacked Andalus in the 9th and 10th centuries were clearly Scandinavian; mostly Norwegians and Danes based in Ireland or enclaves along the French coast. In Latin and Spanish Iberian sources they are usually known by variations on the name Normanni, but sometimes they were called Almajuzes, Almozudes or Almonides, all of which stem from the Arabic word Majus.

On 20 August 844 AD Wahb Allah ibn Hazm, the Arab governor of Al-Ushbuna (Lisbon), reported that fifty-four unknown longships had appeared in the Tagus estuary, plus the same number of smaller vessels. The larger type of ship he called a markib; the smaller a qarib. The raiders came ashore to be challenged by local Muslim militias and garrisons in three fierce battles. After thirteen days of pillaging the surrounding countryside the raiders sailed on. But by now Wahb Allah ibn Hazm's report had reach the capital, Cordoba, and the Umayyad Amir or ruler of Andalus, Abd al-Rahman II (822-852 AD), instructed the military governors of his Atlantic coastal provinces to be on their guard.

Vikings tactics were to find large rivers that enabled them penetrate deep inland with their ships. As a result, when the Vikings reached the broad Guadalquivir most of their fleet sailed up river. Meanwhile other ships landed further south in the province of Shadhuna (now Medina Sidonia).

Their crews made an armed reconnaissance inland and then occupied the ancient port of Cadiz. According to the Arab geographer Al-Bakri, writing in the 11th century, the Moroccan port of Asila was also twice 'attacked' by the Majus, as the Viking raiders were called in Arab sources. The first time was before they attacked Seville and probably involved some of the ships that had taken Cadiz. When the Viking Majus moored near the *ribat,* or coastal fort, that protected Asila's harbour, they announced that they came in peace and would not attack unless they themselves were attacked. They then assembled or purchased from local merchants a large pile of millet that the Vikings clearly needed for food. This suggests that the newcomers knew exactly what they wanted and where to find it. Unfortunately some local Berber tribesmen or nomads saw the millet shining in the sun and thought it was gold! They charged and the Vikings fled to their ships. The Berbers apologised when they found that the bright yellow pile was grain not bullion, but the Vikings said they no longer trusted the Berbers and so sailed off to join in an attack on Seville.

This ceramic plate, probably made in the Balearic Islands in the 11th century AD, shows a three-masted merchant ship of the type used by Islamic Andalusian sailors. This was at least a century before three-masted ships reappeared in Christian European fleets. Andalusians were renowned amongst other Muslims for the size of their transport ships. One reason why such vessels were developed in Andalus may have been that they had to operate in both the Mediterranean and the stormier Atlantic Ocean. (Museo Nazionale di San Matteo, Pisa)

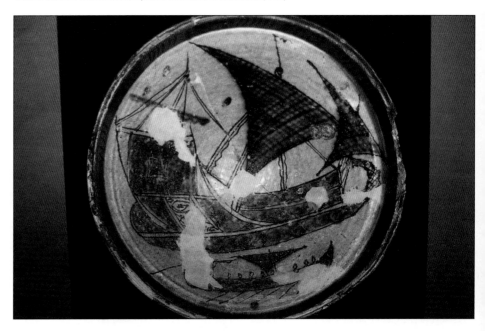

Between Seville and the sea there is a large region of marshes, narrow channels, lagoons and twisting river channels. On 29 September the main Viking force selected the island of Qubtil (now Isla Menor) near the head of the estuary as their base. The island was also an important horse-raising centre and this, as well as its strategic position, must have attracted the Vikings. Next day four ships ventured further upriver, attacked a village today known as Coria del Rio and massacred its inhabitants. The people of Seville soon caught sight of the Vikings' sails that they described as brown, perhaps in contrast to the white canvas sails of Andalusian ships. They tried to organise a defence but Seville was at that time an unfortified city and the local militias could do little. The few ships that they sent against the Vikings were showered with arrows and set on fire, so the bulk of the population fled and the raiders entered Seville. Of those inhabitants left behind, the men, the old and the disabled were slaughtered while women and children were taken captive. The pillage of Seville lasted seven days and the Vikings even tried to burn down the great mosque, though without success.

The Vikings now found that the Guadalquiver was difficult to navigate in late summer and decided not to sail further upstream towards the Umayyad capital of Cordoba. Meanwhile the Umayyad Amir Abd al-Rahman II had hurriedly raised an army to face this sudden assault from an unexpected quarter. The first troops on the scene were light cavalry who used the surrounding hills as bases from which to harass the invaders. Soon, however, they were reinforced by a substantial number of infantry and perhaps some ships.

On 11 November 844 AD, on or around another island in the Guadalquiver called Talayata (today

Tablada, just south of Seville and having an airfield), the Majus were defeated in a bloody river battle. Over a thousand were killed and four hundred taken prisoner to be hanged on gallows and trees within sight of the survivors. On the other hand the Vikings themselves, though now trapped, also had many prisoners so the victorious Andalusians were willing to negotiate. A ransom was agreed and the captives were freed in return for food and clothing rather than booty because the raiders were running seriously short of both. The Vikings were then allowed to sail away in peace, though winter weather probably stopped them leaving before the spring of 845 AD. Thirty of their ships were abandoned, presumably because there were no longer enough men to crew them, and the victors burned these.

Abd al-Rahman II sent the pickled heads of some dead Majus to neighbouring rulers with an announcement that he had defeated these savage sea raiders, but is clear that

not all the Vikings left Andalus. Isolated groups continued to be recorded as bandits around Qarmuna (today Carmona) and Mawrur (today Morón de la Frontera) while others settled on islands in the Guadalquiver estuary. They were eventually pacified by Muhammad ibn Rustum, the general credited with victory at Tablada. Subsequently their descendants converted to Islam, became cattle ranchers and makers of excellent cheese. Meanwhile Abu'l-Fath Nasr, another senior officer who had faced the Vikings along the lower Guadalquivir, rose to high command. He too was a convert to Islam, though as a Christian Andalusian eunuch his origins were more local.

Following the shock of this unexpected invasion, Abd al-Rahman II ordered Seville to be surrounded by a defensive wall, particularly on the river bank, and for observation posts be established along the Atlantic coast. These were manned by Muslim volunteers who would serve time in

'The Second Trumpet' in the a Beatus Commentary on the Apocalypse. This Mozarab (Andalusian Arab Christian) manuscript was made between 922 and 952AD and show four galleys destroyed at the end of the world. Though extremely stylised, these ships have certain interesting characteristics. The most important is their raised boarding beaks rather than low ship-breaking rams. This reflected a change in naval weaponry seen in Mediterranean was-galleys during the early medieval period. (Pierpont Morgan Lib., Ms. 644, f.137r. New York).

The mouth of the great Guadalquiver river near the southern end of the Atlantic coast of the Iberian peninsula. Viking and, of course, Andalusian fleets could not only shelter here but could sail upriver at least as far as Seville. (Author's photograph)

such ribats as a religious duty, keeping watch, praying and, when necessary, fighting the pirates. Immediately after the 844-5 AD attack the Umayyad Andalusian government also started to take a more serious interest in its navy. A much larger and more powerful fleet was constructed, as were shipbuilding facilities and arsenals, of which the most important was in Seville. As a result the Andalusian Umayyads could soon sent a fleet of 300 assorted ships to crush a rebellion in the Balearic Islands in 848-9 AD.

There is strong, though not conclusive, evidence that in 845 AD Abd al-Rahman II also sent a high ranking embassy to what was believed to be the country of 'The King of the Majus.' This might have travelled to king Horik in Denmark, but seems more likely to have gone to the important Viking city of Dublin in Ireland which was dominated by a man called Turgeis.

The head of the Andalusian deputation is said to have been the fifty year old poet and experienced diplomat Yahya ibn Hakam al-Bakri al-Ghazal who had led a similar embassy to the Byzantine Emperor in 840 AD. Their trip took nine perilous months and may have been as much to encourage peaceful trade as to learn more about these fearsome northerners. According to the only surviving later account of his journey, Yahya al-Ghazal sailed to a large island 'three days journey from the mainland' (Britain or Brittany). This island had flowing streams and fine agriculture. Its ruler also controlled the neighbouring 'mainland' and had a wife named Noud (Aud?). Al-Ghazal, as a good Muslim, was shocked but flattered by the way this lady not only made it clear that she found him attractive but that her husband the 'king' did not mind such behaviour! Al-Ghazal even reported that Majus women were free to change their husbands if they were not satisfied.

By the time the Vikings launched a second serious raid against Andalus the Islamic Andalusians, under Muhammad I as Amir of Cordoba (852-886 AD), were ready for them.

Unlike the first raid the leaders of this second Majus fleet are known. They were Björn Ironside, son of Ragnar Lodbrok, and Hastein or Hasting. Both were already well known Viking commanders and their remarkable new expedition may have been seeking fame as much as profit. After raiding northern France and then being besieged by the French on Oissel island for twelve weeks, Björn Ironside was besieged for a second time by a rival Viking leader named Weland who was acting on behalf of the French king. Björn had to pay a large ransom before he and his men were allowed to leave. They then began an epic four-year voyage around the Iberian peninsula, into the Mediterranean and back.

Together with Hastein's ships, this Viking fleet of 858 AD had sixty-two ships but once again it fared badly off northern Spain. The entire coast as far as the French frontier may now have been patrolled by Andalusian vessels and there are suggestions that Andalusian warships even attacked Viking vessels in the Bay of Biscay - effectively in their home waters. They certainly kept watch as far as Cape Finisterre. Driven from the Galician coast by a certain Count Pedro, the Vikings under Björn and Hastein turned south. Some Majus ships sailed ahead of the main fleet as scouts, two of these being intercepted and captured off the Algarve by an Andalusian naval patrol. They were already full of gold, silver, prisoners and supplies so the Viking raiders must already have had some success.

The main fleet pressed on but decided not to sail up the broad Guadalquivir as their unfortunate predecessors had done because a large army, and probably also an Andalusian fleet, defended it. Instead the Vikings attacked Jazirat al-Khadra (today Algeciras). At the time this was the main port on the northern side of the narrow straits; the harbour of Gibraltar not being developed until the 12th century. Björn and Hastein's men plundered Jazirat al-Khadra and burned down the local mosque as a change from destroying churches further north. Once again, however, they were badly cut up by a local Andalusian militia who then built a new mosque whose doors were made from the wood of a captured Viking ship.

The Vikings sailed on through the straits before crossing to the African shore where they had better success at Nakur, the oldest Islamic settlement in Morocco. They were now in the Mediterranean and here, paradoxically, the Viking ships suffered fewer defeats at the hands of Islamic fleets than they and their predecessors had in the Atlantic. This seems strange given the fact that several large and efficient Islamic, Byzantine and even Italian navies were already struggling for domination of the Mediterranean. The Vikings certainly raided the eastern coasts of Andalus, southern France, north and central Italy, probably reaching Alexandria in Egypt and perhaps even ventured into Byzantine waters where, however, their exploits have probably been confused with those of Viking Varangian Rus' arriving via the rivers of Russia.

Inevitably the Viking fleet lost many ships and their epic cruise has been elaborated by several legendary episodes. It is not even entirely clear what route they took home. Some sources seem to suggest that the Vikings sailed up the Ebro river in northern Spain, attacked Pamplona then somehow portaged their surviving ships across the foothills of the Pyrenees before relaunching them into the Bay of Biscay. This was, of course, impossible. In reality the surviving Viking adventurers must have sailed

home the same way they arrived, via the Straits of Gibraltar. Here in 861 AD they again ran the gauntlet of narrow seas patrolled by the Andalusians. They were apparently challenged and lost at least two ships burned. They are also said to have had four ships 'confiscated' by the Andalusians while another forty were lost in a storm off Gibraltar. The idea that fearsome Vikings would have consented to Andalusian customs officials 'confiscating' any ships seems almost as unlikely as hauling such vessels over the Pyrenees. More

probably Björn Ironsides and Hastein were simply beaten in a sea battle.

One of the Andalusian naval patrols which defeated these Vikings, either off the Algarve as they arrived or near the Straits of Gibraltar as they left, was commanded by Khashkhash ibn Sa'id ibn Aswad. He came from a prosperous merchant family from Bajjana (today Pechina near Ameria). Subsequently Khashkhash became even more famous as a leader of the co-called 'Adventurers of Lisbon' who made a number of voyages far into the north Atlantic and

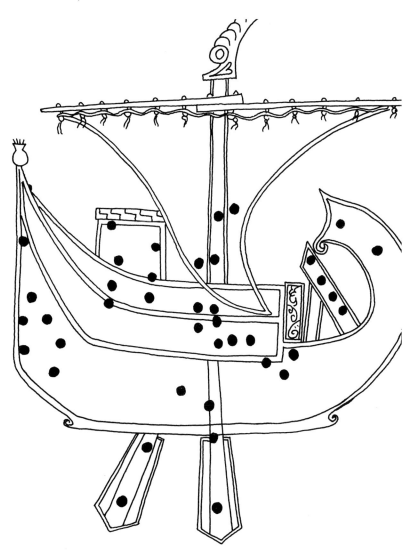

'Argo' in a copy of the Kitab al-Sufar *or Book of Fixed Stars by Al-Sufi. It was made in 1224 AD in Sabta, now the Spanish-ruler port of Ceuta, on the northernmost tip of Morocco. Again this highly stylized representation of a ship includes features which are not seen in copies of the Kitab al-Sufar made further east, though some do appear in other Middle Eastern illustration of ships. Significantly, perhaps, these features are not seen in medieval western or northern European pictures. The most interesting are keel extensions or 'runners' at the bow and stern. (Vatican Library, Ms. Ross 1033, Rome)*

The Guardiana river seen from the castle of Mertola in southern Portugal. Even in the high summer, as seen here, the Guardiana was broad and might have provided Viking raiders with a route deep into Andalus. (Author's photograph)

southwards along the African coast. They, like their Portuguese successors in the great Age of European Discovery, were almost certainly trying to open up new trade routes.

Meanwhile the surviving Viking ships had sailed round the Atlantic coast and it was almost certainly when they reached the vicinity of what is now San Sebastian that they launched a final raid inland towards Pamplona. One way or another the Vikings captured King García Iñíguez whom they subsequently released for a huge ransom. Apparently the Vikings had already raided Galicia to the west where they captured a certain Sa'dun al-Surunbaki. He had been a companion of Abd al-Rahman ibn Marwan al-Jilliki, the leader of a revolt against the Umayyads in alliance with the Christian kingdom of Asturias. Sa'dun al-Surunbaki was himself ransomed from the Vikings by a Jewish merchant and spent the rest of his life as a brigand around Coimbra and Santarem in what is today Portugal. Some time in 862 AD the remaining Majus ships returned to their starting point in the estuary of the Loire in France, after a four year voyage which must rate as one of the most extraordinary exploits in Viking history.

Vikings would not reappear on the Andalusian coast for another seventy or so years, but their first two raids were already famous in the far north. They also some rather strange results. Björn Ironside and Hastein sold most of their prisoners for ransom but some unfortunates were kept because of their exotic appearance. These included black African, or very dark-skinned Saharan Berbers, captured at Nakur. Some ended up in Ireland where they were mentioned in early

Irish annals as *fir gorm* 'blue men' or *blámenn* 'black men.' When the Irish retook Limerick from the Vikings their booty also included a magnificent Moorish saddle and coloured silk garments from the Islamic lands. For his part Hastein, or Hasting, remained an important leader of the Loire Vikings for another thirty years; almost achieving the status of a local king.

In 964 AD the Caliph, as he now claimed to be, of Cordoba, Hakam II (961-976 AD) personally inspected the naval base at Al-Mariya (today Almeria), the Umayyad fleet of over three hundred ships and a nearby ribat fully manned by religious volunteers. He was probably concerned about a threat from the rival Fatimid Caliphs based in North Africa but Al-Hakam's naval preparations also meant that the Andalusians were prepared when a new Viking fleet suddenly appeared in the Atlantic two years later.

Part of a carved ivory box made in Cuenca in Islamic Andalus in 1026 AD. The box comes from the Treasury of the Monastery of Santo Domingo do Silos and illustrates huntsmen on horseback and on foot. This particular infantry archer, with his composite bow and mail hauberk, must reflect the men who fought on board Andalusian warships in the Atlantic. (Archaeological Museum, Burgos)

This third major attack was carried out by pagan Danes whom Richard I, Duke of Normandy, had urged in the direction of Spain in order to rid him of their embarrassing presence. At first they reportedly attacked the Christian coasts of northern Spain. Then, on 23rd June 966 AD, the Caliph Al-Hakam II received a message from the governor of Qasr Abi Danis (also called Qasr Banu Wardas; today Alcacer do Sol) stating that a fleet of twenty-eight ships had been seen in the area. As these Vikings ravaged the region around Lisbon, a local Andalusian force was sent against them. Both sides suffered heavily in the subsequent battle and the Vikings took many prisoners. Meanwhile an Andalusian fleet from Seville set sail and found the Viking ships off the mouth of the river of Shilb (today Silves; actually the estuary of the rivers Odelouca and Arade). Many Viking vessels were destroyed and Muslim prisoners rescued.

The surviving Viking ships fled, though news continued to reach Cordoba concerning their activities along the Atlantic coast. The Andalusian fleet returned to the Guadalquivir and, although the Majus had been driven off, the continuing threat was serious enough for the Caliph Al-Hakam II to order his admiral, Ibn Futays, to keep the fleet in readiness. According to the Moroccan historian Ibn 'Idari al-Marrakusi:

That same year Al-Hakam ordered Ibn Futays to … construct ships of the same type as those used by the Majus, may God curse them, in the hope that they would approach his ships.

Although the Andalusians might well have hoped to lure future raiders into close-quarter combat, they may also have hoped to emulate the ocean-going capabilities of Viking ships.

In the event the Scandinavians did not return, at least not in strength. In 970 AD some Vikings attacked Galicia and briefly occupied the Christian

Part of another carved ivory box made for prince Abdl al-Malik al-Muzaffar in 1005 AD. Light cavalry such as the swordsman and spearman shown here were amongst the most effective Andalusian troops facing Viking raiders in the 9th and 10th centuries. (Cathedral Treasure, Pamplona)

sacred city of Santiago de Compostella. Some may have remained in this area and have been responsible for alarming reports of numerous Danish ships off the Atlantic Andalusian coast late in June 971 AD. This time the Caliph Al-Hakam II ordered the commander of his Mediterranean fleet, Abd al-Rahman ibn Muhammad ibn al-Rumahis, to join the Atlantic fleet at Seville. They then jointly patrolled the Atlantic coast though on this occasion the Vikings did not venture ashore. A somewhat unreliable later account describes Vikings landing in the Tagus estuary or Lisbon in June 972 AD where they were defeated by the joint Atlantic and Mediterranean fleet. This same source also mentions an Andalusian army which went to the Algarve, then marched northwards to Shantarin (today Santarem) and back to Corbova between June and September 972 AD in what may have been the last known Viking raid on Andalusian territory.

The Umayyad state, and to a lesser extent the Christian principalities of the north, had proved themselves militarily effective against the Viking threat. They had fleets, fortifications and well-organised armies. The peoples of the Iberian peninsula also had naval capabilities which enabled them to face Scandinavian pirate fleets at sea as well as on land; something few other early medieval peoples could do. As far as the Vikings themselves were concerned, these raids were led by freebooters rather than Scandinavian rulers, and were mostly carried out by men from coastal enclaves on the French coast. It is also important to remember that during such long distance voyages Vikings ships would probably not have carried more than thirty men, unlike the more crowded ships used in short range Nordic raiding. Perhaps as a result those Vikings who raided Andalus tended to be beaten when they came up against a proper defending army.

Soldiers defending a walled town in a Mozarab copy of the Beatus Commentary on the Apocalypse, *dating from the 11th century. They are using spears, bows and perhaps grenades filled with* naft *or Greek Fire. (Cathedral Archive, Gerona, Cod. 242)*

On land Viking raiders tried to seize horses whenever the could and constructed bases, sometimes fortified with earth and timber, on islands or other such defensible locations close to their ships. In battle they almost inevitably relied on infantry drawn up behind a 'shield wall' and probably supported by archers using longbows. When not actually raiding, their tactics appear static and old fashioned. Andalusian armies, in contrast, were heirs to a highly sophisticated Islamic military tradition which drew upon the heritage of the Semitic Middle East, the Roman and Byzantine Empire, the Sassanian Persian Empire and to a lesser extent India. Islamic armies further east were also learning from the Turks and even Chinese, though these latter influences had not yet reached Andalus. Furthermore Arab-Islamic Andalus was a highly structured state with a sophisticated bureaucracy, administration, taxation, communications and widespread literacy. Its armies were large, effective, frighteningly disciplined in the eyes of their Christian rivals, and well equipped. In battle they relied on close co-ordination between generally lightly armoured cavalry and infantry. The latter included archers and javelin throwers in steady ranks, as well as highly developed pyrotechnics. Small wonder, then, that the Viking raiders fared badly in open battle against such opponents.

The Andalusians' successes against the Vikings at sea seem, at first glance, more surprising. Viking ships and seafaring skills were undoubtedly the finest in the Atlantic while many if not most of the Andalusians would have been relative newcomers from the Mediterranean. Some Andalusian sailors and perhaps commanders would have had experience of the Atlantic, but it was not yet their natural element. Andalusian fighting ships were *shini* galleys and, although some may have been more strongly built with a higher freeboard to cope with the open ocean, there is little evidence that they differed much from normal Mediterranean galleys. These in turn had developed from earlier Roman galleys. But they were more strongly built than their predecessors and had boarding beaks on their prows rather than the low-lying ship-breaking rams of earlier naval warfare. Some centuries later Genoese, Venetian and Spanish galleys would appear in the Bay of Biscay, the English Channel and North Sea where they proved themselves to be the most effective warships of their day. Such vessels were certainly stronger and in some cases larger than the ordinary medieval Mediterranean galley, but how far the Andalusians had taken this development is unknown.

Nevertheless in fair weather a shini galley under oars would have been able to outmanoeuvre a Viking longship in narrow water. A typical Arab shini of the eastern Mediterranean carried from 140 to 180 oarsmen, up to 150 marines, and had one or more superstructures which gave it a height advantage in battle, particularly when using *naft* or Greek Fire. The oarsmen were volunteers, not slaves, and, unlike the oarsmen in rival Byzantine galleys, they were expected to fight. Sailors and marines were commanded by officers who had recognised ranks, just like those in Islamic armies. Other evidence, again from the Arab Mediterranean, shows that galleys fought in crescent or in more compact formations, used feigned retreat and launched ambushes from behind islands. If these capabilities were brought into the Atlantic, and if the weather was fair enough for shini galleys to operate freely, then it is

An army of infantry and cavalry in a Mozarab copy of the Beatus Commentary on the Apocalypse, *dating from the 10th century. There is no sign of these men wearing armour, though of course it could be hidden beneath their clothing. On the other hand most Andalusian soldiers were lightly equipped, which enabled them to react to sudden Viking attacks with great speed. (Archivo Capitulra, Seo de Urgel).*

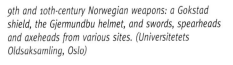

9th and 10th-century Norwegian weapons: a Gokstad shield, the Gjermundbu helmet, and swords, spearheads and axeheads from various sites. (Universitetets Oldsaksamling, Oslo)

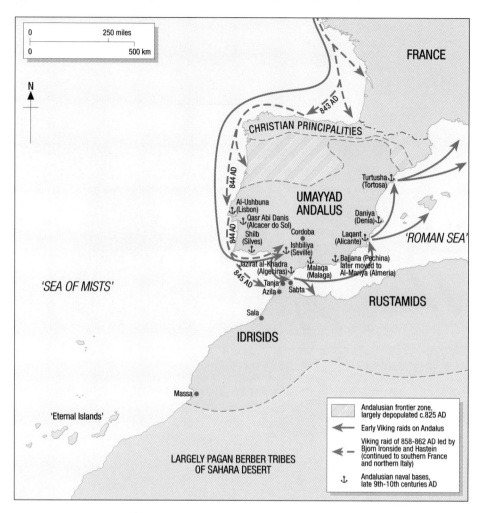

The Iberian Peninsula and North-West Africa, 800–1000 AD.

The map legend reads:

- Andalusian frontier zone, largely depopulated c.825 AD
- Early Viking raids on Andalus
- Viking raid of 858-862 AD led by Björn Ironside and Hastein (continued to southern France and northern Italy)
- Andalusian naval bases, late 9th-10th centuries AD

hardly surprising that the Vikings got a bloody nose, especially if caught in a river estuary by a superior number of Andalusian galleys.

Some scholars have described the Viking raids on the Iberian peninsula as 'famous but wildly speculative operations.' They could also be described as long-range experiments that did not succeed. The expedition to Seville in 844 AD resulted in a particularly bloody repulse while that of Björn and Hastein set out with sixty-two ships but came back with twenty or so. Both failed because the defences of well established states were fully capable of dealing with pinprick Viking raids. This was even truer of the second phase of Viking attacks in the mid-10th century AD.

The sudden Viking assault and the terror it they inspired were, however, long remembered in Andalusian Arabic literature. They also stimulated a greater interest in the northern lands. Even if the embassy of Yahya ibn Hakam al-Bakri al-Ghazal was a later myth, the information contained in a 13th century report of this supposed visit reflects accurate Andalusian knowledge of the Vikings and their homelands. It correctly reported that Christianity was spreading amongst the Vikings while old-fashioned fire-worshippers tended to be confined to outlying regions or islands. The Viking Majus were also known to be essentially the same people at the Scandinavian Rus' who made their way to the central and eastern Islamic lands via Russia.

A comparable degree of knowledge was not apparent in the opposite direction. In the British Isles, for example, the Muslims of Andalusia played a prominent role in a famous early English epic tale, King Horn, which survives in a slightly later medieval form. Here, however, these 'Saracens' are portrayed as cruel men from the sea who invade Westire (Ireland) before being defeated almost single-handedly by the hero Horn. In fact English and Irish memories of Viking brutality had been shifted to those Islamic peoples who, by the 12th and 13th centuries, had become the new bogeymen of Christian Europe. Nevertheless, hidden in King Horn, there may be dim recollections of Andalusian merchants, fishermen, whaler hunters and otherwise unrecorded maritime rivals.

SOURCES

Christides, V., 'Milaha' (navigation, seamanship) in Encyclopedia of Islam, 2nd edition, vol. VII (Leiden 1991) pp. 40-46

Dunlop, D. M., 'al-Bahr al-Muhit,' (Encircling Sea, including the Atlantic) in Encyclopedia of Islam, 2nd edition, vol. I (Leiden 1960) p. 934

Dunlop, D. M., 'Djaza'ir al-Khalida,' (Canary Islands, etc.) in Encyclopedia of Islam, 2nd edition, vol. II (Leiden 1965) p. 522

Dunlop, D. M., 'The British Isles according to Medieval Arabic Authors,' Islamic Quarterly IV (1957) pp. 11-28

Griffith, P., The Viking Art of War (London 1995)

Jones, G., A History of the Vikings (Oxford 1968)

Lévi-Provençal, E., Histoire de l'Espagne Musulmane, 3 vols. (Paris 1950-1967)

Lévi-Provençal, E., L'Espagne Musulmane au Xème Siècle (Paris 1932).

Melvinger, A., 'Al-Madjus,' in Encyclopedia of Islam, 2nd edition, vol. V (Leiden 1986) pp. 1118-1121

Melvinger, A., Les premières incursions des Vikings en Occident d'après les sources arabes (Uppsala 1955)

Munis, H., 'Contribution à l'étude des invasions des Normands en Espagne' Bulletin de la Société Royale d'Etudes Historiques, Egypte vol. II/1 (1950)

Nicolle, D., 'Shipping in Islamic Art: Seventh Through Sixteenth Century AD' American Neptune XLIX (1989) pp. 168-197.

Oxenstierna, E., trans. C. Hunter, The Norsemen (London 1966).

ABOUT THE AUTHOR

Dr David Nicolle worked in the BBC Arabic Service, gained an MA from the School of Oriental and Asian Studies and a PhD from Edinburgh University. He taught world and Islamic art at Yarmuk University, Jordan, and is one of Osprey's most prolific and popular authors. He has contributed more than 20 titles to the series and is currently working on Men-at-Arms 348: The Moors, due for publication in January 2001.

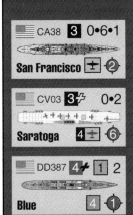

The siege and battle of Nagashino in 1575 together make up one of the pivotal events in samurai history. The army of the Takeda clan, who had been besieging the tiny but stubbornly defended fortress for nearly ten days, abandoned their siege lines to assault the army sent by Oda Nobunaga to relieve Nagashino. The great strength of the Takeda was the immense striking power of their cavalry, but when they swept down upon the enemy lines they found themselves faced by 3,000 arquebusiers who had been trained to fire in organised volleys, and who were protected by a loose palisade. The gunfire broke the impact of the initial charge, and as the second wave of horsemen prepared to go in, the gunners calmly reloaded under the protection of their spearmen. Once again the line held, and when the Takeda faltered for a third time the samurai and footsoldiers of the Oda began to engage the attackers in hand to hand fighting. Several hours of conflict followed, at the end of which the Takeda withdrew after taking enormous casualties, broken forever as a military and political influence in Japan.

In a very real sense the brief transition between the siege of Nagashino being ended and the battle of Nagashino beginning, a period of time lasting but a few hours, marks an important turning point in the development of samurai warfare. The siege had been a classic of the old style. It was conducted against a traditional and simple style of fortress built from wood and some stone that included in its defence a modest number of arquebuses and only one cannon. Attacks upon it had involved an assault party on a raft floated down the river, mining on the landward side, fire arrows loosed against the wooden buildings, but, above all, repeated assaults on the walls with hand-to-hand fighting. By contrast, the battle which followed a few hours afterwards was the herald of a military revolution, whereby a straightforward tactical charge, the sort that had given the Takeda victories at Uedahara in 1548 and Mikata ga hara in 1572, was stunted by what was in effect a new type of field fortress that combined organised gunfire on a large scale with simple defence works. From this point on Japanese warfare, in particular Japanese defensive warfare, would never be quite the same again. Therefore, although the Nagashino campaign began with a siege, I shall argue that it is to the combination of the guns and fences of the Nagashino battlefield, not the old fashioned stockades and towers of the Nagashino castle, that we must look if we are to understand what brought about the revolution in castle design and warfare that Japan was to see over the next fifty years.

Japanese Castles and the lessons of Nagashino

STEPHEN TURNBULL

The battle of Shizugatake, from a painted screen in Osaka castle. Although the details of the castle successive sculpted baileys that followed the mountain's contours is well illustrated. (© Japan Archi

THE EVOLUTION OF THE JAPANESE CASTLE

The type of Japanese castle design that Nagashino's fortress represented already had a long history. As the Japanese landscape has always had a shortage of stone and an abundance of trees clustered on forested mountains, it was natural that it should be the latter two factors – timber and high ground, which determined the character of Japanese fortifications for many centuries. The first Japanese castles, therefore, consisted of simple wooden stockades linking towers and gates that followed the natural defences provided by the height and the contours of the mountains from which the materials for the wooden walls had been taken. The erection of palisades on top of earth works, raised by excavating a forward ditch, could compensate for the lack of high ground when a position had to be erected in an area of flatlands, but such topography was avoided wherever possible. It was from the mountain-top *yamashiro* (mountain castles) of Akasaka and Chihaya, which were built on these principles, that the famous Kusunoki Masashige conducted his spirited defensive campaigns and guerrilla actions between 1331 and 1336.

Such designs persisted on into the *Sengoku-jidai*, the Period of Warring States, which is commonly accepted as beginning with the Ônin War of 1467-76. As central authority collapsed those who had been the Shogun's deputies out in the provinces took the territories they had governed and made them their own. In this they were challenged, and frequently overthrown, by a new breed of warlord who owed nothing to ancient privilege and prestige and everything to their skills in warfare. These men, the first *daimyô* (great names), led armies and ruled territories whose borders were defined solely by their latest conquests, and to defend their lands they adopted the yamashiro model on a huge scale. From one *honjô* (headquarters castle), a network of satellite castles radiated out, each of which had its own smaller sub-satellite, and with each sub-satellite having its own local cluster of tiny guard posts. The network would often also be linked visually by a chain of fire beacons.

For a daimyô's honjô, and for most of the satellite castles, a simple stockade was not enough to withstand enemy attack or to provide barracks space for a garrison, so a technique developed whereby the mountain on which the yamashiro stood was literally carved up. Using the formidable resources in manpower that a successful daimyô could now command, neighbouring mountains were sculpted into a series of interlocking baileys which followed the natural lines only in the sense that the contours provided the guide for the excavation of wide, flat horizontal surfaces, each overlooked by the

The traditional Japanese yamashiro, which made use of the height advantage supplied by nature, is shown most dramatically by this view looking down from the walls of Japan's highest yamashiro, the castle of Bitchu-Matsuyama. (© Japan Archive)

one above it. The result was a gigantic and bizarre earthwork produced by removing materials rather than piling them up. Some of these highly developed yamashiro could be as much as 200km long, but height was often a more important consideration than width, with successive baileys covering huge areas at different levels. Garrisons could number up to 2,000 men. On top of this framework were placed fences, towers, stables, storehouses, walkways, bridges, gates and usually a rudimentary version of a castle keep. Very little stone was used in the construction except for strengthening the bases of gatehouses and towers and to combat soil erosion from the excavated slopes. As time went by the simple palisades and towers inside the yamashiro were replaced by stronger wattle and daub walls, plastered over against fire attack and roofed with tiles as a protection against rain.

By the time of the battle of Nagashino it had also been realised that if the cut away slopes of the natural hills were reinforced with tightly packed stones arranged scientifically so that any weight upon them was dissipated outwards and downwards, then much larger, taller and heavier buildings could be successfully raised on top of them. In some cases artificial mounds were built in this way on flat areas and encased with stone. The result was the beginning of the construction of the earliest form of the castle keeps that are now such an attractive feature of extant Japanese military architecture. It is, however, important to realise that it was the huge overlapping walls made from the carved stone-clad hillsides, rather than any buildings added on top of them, that were the fundamental defining feature of a Japanese castle. The huge tower keeps that now grace such castles as Himeji and Matsumoto were by no means a universal element. The earliest tower keeps date only from the 1570s, and many were not added until early in the seventeenth century. It can also be shown from sources such as painted screens of battle exploits that the majority of the keeps that withstood attack during the time of civil wars would have been of much simpler construction than these magnificent towers.

FROM NAGASHINO TO AZUCHI

Firearms had been used in Japanese warfare from the late 1540s onwards, but had produced no visible impact in castle design by the time of the siege of Nagashino. None of Nagashino's defences were designed in any way for specific protection against gunfire, or to allow the use of gunfire rather than arrows in defence. It is also unlikely that Nagashino possessed a keep in any form other than a simple two storey wooden building with a Japanese style curving roof, but in one respect Nagashino castle was exceptionally fortunate. It was not built upon a stripped out mountain, but very literally founded on solid rock, a dramatic promontory that marked the confluence of two minor rivers that joined at Nagashino to become the mighty Toyokawa. These rocky cliffs therefore formed two sides of an equilateral triangle, which was completed on its third side by an outer bailey of a simple ditch, mound and palisade construction.

This combination of two impregnable rocky sides and the sheer determination of the defenders behind the wall of the third side kept every ingenious Takeda attack at bay, and forced the commander Takeda Katsuyori to settle down for what could be a long wait until the defenders surrendered from starvation. Up to this point the siege of Nagashino had been little different, except in intensity, from a hundred similar actions fought elsewhere in Japan. But then the situation changed. A brave warrior called Torii Sune'emon slipped out of the castle and took a message to Oda Nobunaga, who immediately set out with a relief army. But Nobunaga did not simply fall precipitately on to the rear of the

Here the siege lines at Nagashino are seen in close up. There are bundles of green bamboo and wooden shields from which the weary Takeda footsoldiers shoot arrows and fire guns. Three Takeda generals join them. Anayama Nobukimi, who is also a monk, Sanada Nobutsuna and the veteran Yamagata Masakage, whose hair is white. (© 2000 Osprey Publishing Ltd. from Campaign 69 Nagashino 1575 by Stephen Turnbull, illustration by Howard Gerrard)

Takeda lines. Instead he halted on a low ridge a few kilometres away. It had a forest to its rear and left, a stream in front, and a river to its right. With the aid of wooden stakes and the massed ranks of his gunners Nobunaga converted the site into an instant castle, and waited for the historic and doomed attack.

The battle of Nagashino was therefore won not from behind the walls of a castle, but from a simple position constructed overnight and defended by guns. So to the trends already visible in the design of those Japanese castles faced with stone that were intended to be permanent bases

was added another: the lesson of the effectiveness of something created both temporarily and quickly, and it is remarkable that the development and dissemination of both these strands should be so closely associated with one man: Oda Nobunaga. His successful deployment of firearms was to have a great bearing on both trends, and within a year of Nagashino Japan was to see the first, and perhaps the finest, of the new style permanent military bases/palaces in Nobunaga's castle of Azuchi. This remarkable fortress demonstrated Nobunaga's power in several ways. First, it showed the remarkable effects that could be

produced by encasing the excavated hills of a yamashiro in shaped and cut stone. No bare earthen walls were now visible. All was graceful sloping stone, and as well as providing their own defences, these cyclopean mounds allowed the raising of a spectacular seven storey keep ornamented within and without as befitted the grandeur to which Nobunaga now aspired.

Around Azuchi's keep were a score of smaller towers, each of which would have done credit as the main keep for a normal sized castle, but Azuchi was huge, built to house the enormous garrison (over 10,000 men)

Japanese castles and the European parallel

In Medieval Europe the trend in castle building had been to build up, allowing the walls to rise as high as possible so that an assailant's siege towers and scaling ladders would have to be impossibly long. Japanese castle technology, prior to the introduction of the tower keep in the 1570s, did not allow a similar use of height through buildings. Instead height was provided by nature through the yamashiro model, and as another means of keeping an enemy at bay the Japanese also went for width, joining neighbouring hills together in a complex of encircling baileys. In this way Japan anticipated Europe, because the advent of siege artillery in Europe led to a rapid change in priorities. High medieval walls were too vulnerable to cannon fire. One solution was to add width to height, so that European fortresses grew into enormous complexes. Another solution was to pile up earth behind these walls or inside towers to increase their thickness. Unfortunately, when breaches were made the earth that fell out provided an easy slope for an assailant to climb. This problem was solved with the introduction of the model of low, squat and very thick walls intended primarily for artillery. The lower walls, of course, made assault that much easier, so instead of high corner towers lower, quadrilateral angle bastions were introduced, from where fire could be directed along the flanks of the building against scaling parties, leaving no blind spots.

The Japanese experience provides an exact parallel. Projecting towers and walls, easily recognisable as bastions, were added to the Japanese castle and were referred to picturesquely as *koguchi* (tigers' mouths). Alternatively, or in addition, a long wall could be concertinaed into a design known as by *bu* (folding screen). Both allowed the important flanking fire from hundreds of arquebuses. In front of the European bastions would be a wide ditch, just as in many Japanese examples, with a slope (the glacis) running down towards the besiegers' lines. This was the castle design that became known as the *trace italienne* (the Italian system) because the style first appeared during the Spanish wars in Italy. The size of its ditches and walls, and the deployment of sharpshooters with arquebuses was intended to keep a besiegers' own artillery as far away as possible. This European technique of low and squat fortresses whose stone walls were packed behind with earth thus unconsciously imitated the Japanese design, which used the same technique in reverse by excavating a mountain and encasing it in stone, so within a few years European fortresses began to look more like Japanese ones. Also, although Europe possessed more and heavier cannon than Japan for many years, both models were defended primarily by gunpowder weapons, with arquebuses predominating in Japan.

that few daimyô could afford to feed or to arm. Nobunaga could do both, and the internal walls of Azuchi were fitted with numerous racks for hundred of arquebuses, which could be quickly lifted down and poked out through the windows and weapon slits of the towers, all cunningly designed to provide flanking fire from projecting bastions. Azuchi, therefore, may also be regarded as Japan's first artillery fortress, where gunfire was the primary defence, and with its construction Nobunaga demonstrated how his understanding of the use of gunpowder weapons united both battlefield and fortified place.

CASTLES AND THE NAGASHINO BATTLEFIELD

The second trend associated with Oda Nobunaga, that of using a temporary field fortification either to augment a castle of replace it, continued to influence castle design in parallel with the first strand described above. The rapid dissemination of this second trend can be directly linked to Nagashino, because by strange coincidence the roll call of Oda Nobunaga's army included many of the men who were to be enormously influential in the following years of samurai history. Toyotomi Hideyoshi, Tokugawa Ieyasu and Shibata Katsuie

The Uto tower of Kumamoto castle, the only tower in the complex to have survived in its original state. It is of wood painted black rather than the conventional white. The Uto tower is believed to have been the original keep of Uto castle, which was owned by Konishi Yukinaga. It was taken down and moved to Kumamoto as a secondary tower. (© Japan Archive)

are but three of the movers and shakers of Japanese history who fought shoulder to shoulder at Nagashino and then went on to fight each other with the lessons of Nagashino having been learned dramatically at first hand.

When the battle ended Oda Nobunaga returned to his base at Gifu

This woodblock print shows a siege in action. Much use is made of guns, particularly from the gatehouse. (© Japan Archive)

The inter-relationship between Himeji's magnificent keep, its inner walls and its moat is seen here in this view of Himeji at cherry blossom time. (© Japan Archive)

with much unfinished business to deal with. At the top of his agenda was the final destruction of the warrior monks of the Ikkô-ikki, whose early adoption of firearms had been a precursor to Nagashino. Nobunaga himself had experienced the effects of the mass use of arquebuses at their hands during an attack on their fortified cathedral of Ishiyama Honganji. This, combined with Nobunaga's own earlier experiments with rolling volleys, had led directly to his battlefield layout at Nagashino. Over the next few years the newly confident Nobunaga literally met fire with fire, overcoming the warrior monks finally in 1580. By now Oda Nobunaga had perfected the technique of rotational volley firing, ten years before the idea first emerged in Europe, where the technique is attributed to Count William Louis of Nassau, who set it out (including diagrams) in a letter to his cousin Maurice of Nassau in 1594. He called it the European countermarch, and said that he obtained the idea by

studying the similar tactics of missile troops in the Roman legions. Meanwhile Takeda Katsuyori, the loser at Nagashino, showed the lesson that the battle had been for him by making a major strategic U-turn. For half a century the Takeda had won and controlled territory without ever building anything that could be described as a headquarters castle. Tsutsujigasaki, the Takeda capital, was a mansion built on flat ground with little other than a moat and a fence for protection. As Nobunaga's armies closed in on his home province Katsuyori abandoned Tsutsujigasaki for the stone walls of newly built Shimpu. His retainers saw it as a very bad omen, a prophecy that came true with Katsuyori's defeat and death in 1582.

Oda Nobunaga himself followed Katsuyori as a Guest in the 'White Jade Pavilion' before the year was out, and in 1583 his successor Toyotomi Hideyoshi was to be found fighting his former Nagashino comrade in arms Shibata Katsuie at the battle of Shizugatake. Katsuie's general Sakuma Morimasa, another Nagashino veteran, had besieged the mountain fortress of Shizugatake,

which, like Nagashino, was holding out stubbornly. On being informed that Sakuma had not abandoned his siege lines for the security of one or other of the yamashiro that he had successfully captured, Toyotomi Hideyoshi advanced on Shizugatake in a rapid forced march. Sakuma's position was Nagashino in reverse. Expecting no response from Hideyoshi for several days he had stayed in the siege lines. Hideyoshi fell upon him before he had a chance to erect any form of field fortifications, and soon his entire army was defeated.

Such a failure to benefit from the first hand experience of Nagashino was not shared by Tokugawa Ieyasu, who was the next rival to challenge Hideyoshi for supremacy. Their territories met in Owari province, formerly the Oda heartlands, and it was the way in which their antagonism was resolved that was to show the most dramatic influence from the Nagashino experience. Owari province (much of which now lies within the boundaries of the city of Nagoya) was largely flat, so Ieyasu took the opportunity to secure one of the few pieces of high ground, which was the site of the former castle of

The angle bastions of the inner moat of Osaka castle, showing how flanking fire could be delivered exactly as in the design of the European 'trace italienne'. (© Japan Archive)

Chronology

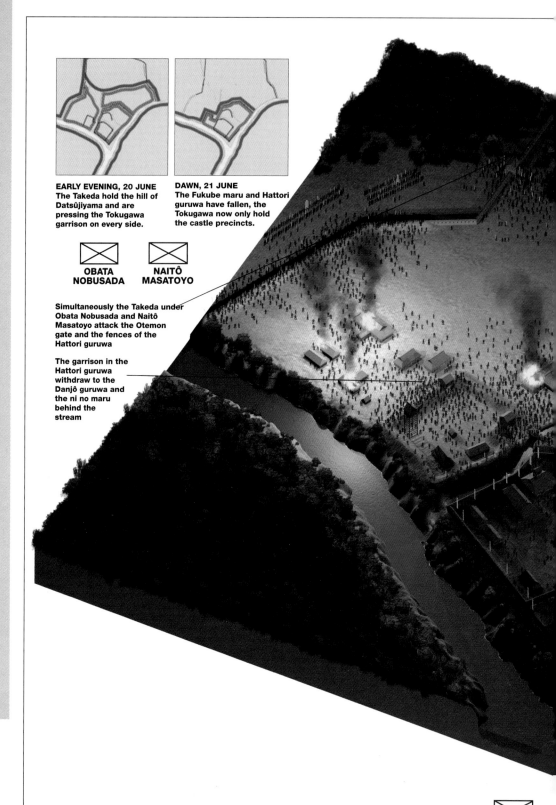

EARLY EVENING, 20 JUNE
The Takeda hold the hill of
Datsûjiyama and are
pressing the Tokugawa
garrison on every side.

DAWN, 21 JUNE
The Fukube maru and Hattori
guruwa have fallen, the
Tokugawa now only hold
the castle precincts.

**OBATA
NOBUSADA**

**NAITÔ
MASATOYO**

Simultaneously the Takeda under
Obata Nobusada and Naitô
Masatoyo attack the Otemon
gate and the fences of the
Hattori guruwa

The garrison in the
Hattori guruwa
withdraw to the
Danjô guruwa and
the ni no maru
behind the
stream

**OKUDAIRA
SADAMASA**

THE ATTACKS ON NAGASHINO
CASTLE, 20–21 JUNE 1575

On the nght of 20 June the Takeda forces launched an attack on the castle
from two sides, these attacks carried on until the dawn of the 21st.

*Bird's Eye View 1 from 'Nagashino 1575'
showing the night attack on the castle –
with original caption.*

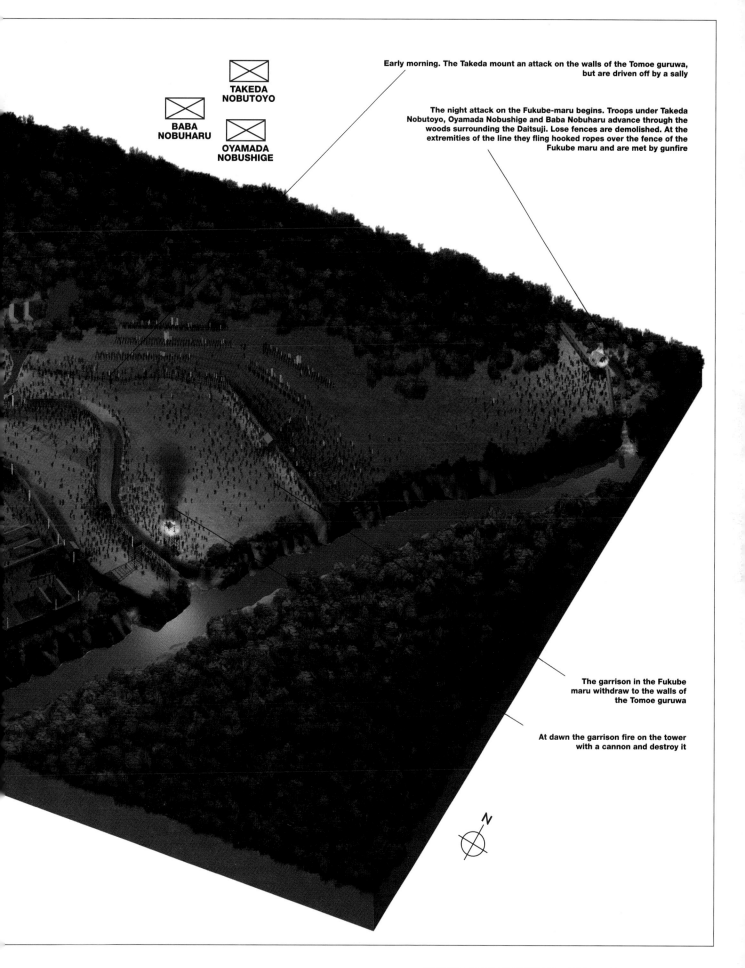

TAKEDA
NOBUTOYO

BABA
NOBUHARU

OYAMADA
NOBUSHIGE

Early morning. The Takeda mount an attack on the walls of the Tomoe guruwa, but are driven off by a sally

The night attack on the Fukube-maru begins. Troops under Takeda Nobutoyo, Oyamada Nobushige and Baba Nobuharu advance through the woods surrounding the Daitsuji. Lose fences are demolished. At the extremities of the line they fling hooked ropes over the fence of the Fukube maru and are met by gunfire

The garrison in the Fukube maru withdraw to the walls of the Tomoe guruwa

At dawn the garrison fire on the tower with a cannon and destroy it

N

The keep of Sunchon castle, the finest example of the Japanese castle style buit hurriedly in Korea. (© Japan Archive)

Komaki, 86 metres above sea level. As time was pressing Ieyasu's men took to the spade, and raised earth ramparts as Komaki's defences in a few days. Four other forts were also strengthened to provide secure communications to the south and west.

Hideyoshi soon heard of Ieyasu's activities and responded in kind. Neither of his two frontline forts of Iwasakiyama and Nijubori had Komaki's advantage of high ground, so, with memories of Nagashino behind him, he ordered the construction of a long rampart to join the two together. The resulting earthwork, probably strengthened with wood, was completed overnight. It was 2km long, 4.1m high and 2.2m thick, and pierced with several gates to allow a counter attack. The slope of the rampart no doubt also allowed for the provision of firing positions.

Satisfied with his Nagashino-like front line, Hideyoshi set up his headquarters to the rear at Gakuden. The following morning, upon observing Hideyoshi's rampart, Ieyasu immediately ordered a similar line to be constructed parallel to it and out from Komaki to the south-east. This was a more modest construction only 800 metres long and anchored on the small fort of Hachimanzuka, from where it was a short distance to his communications forts of Hira and Kobata, but the result was that these two veterans of Nagashino were now facing each other from behind the sixteenth-century equivalent of a First World War trench system.

It was almost inevitable that the lessons of Nagashino should not only have caused these highly skilled generals to take the defensive measures that they did, but should also prevent either of them from making the first move in attacking each other. The result was stalemate, which was not a situation at all conducive to the samurai spirit, and within a few days there occurred the bloody but indecisive battle of Nagakute. However, Nagakute was not fought between the Komaki lines, but arose from an attempt by one of Hideyoshi's generals to raid Ieyasu's home province while he was sitting in the ramparts of Komaki. Nagakute having been fought some distance away, both armies returned to their lines, and the stalemate began again. Once more boredom set in, and this time it was relieved by Hideyoshi withdrawing more men to besiege Ieyasu's ally Oda Nobuo in his castle of Kagenoi. In fact no frontal attack between the two ever took place at Komaki, and eventually their differences were settled by negotiation and the ramparts were allowed to crumble back into the rice fields.

The next example of the use of earthworks combined with guns is to be found during Hideyoshi's invasion of Korea in 1592. The rapid advance of the Japanese up the Korean peninsula stalled following the capture of P'yong-yang, which had been defended by stone walls built in the usual Korean pattern of a long, vertical but narrow construction, not based round an earth core as in the Japanese style. When P'yong-yang came under threat from the expeditionary army sent by the Ming Chinese the Japanese defenders made no attempt to increase the size of the Korean walls. Instead they turned to digging to augment the existing defences of the city by horizontal earthwork bastions. P'yong-yang therefore provides the first example of the construction of recognisable Japanese-style fortifications in Korea. The advancing Chinese, who compared the Japanese efforts unfavourably to their own magnificent Great Wall of China, scorned the crude ramparts, referring to them as 'earth-caverns', and likened them to the primitive earthworks found among the Jurchids of Manchuria. What the Chinese did not realise was that these earth caverns' were designed to provide a clear field of fire for thousands of arquebuses, and to absorb whatever punishment the Chinese cannon could throw at them. In spite of a massive assault by the Chinese army the huge earthworks absorbed all their artillery fire. Those who fought their way to P'yong-yang's gates were then enticed inside and cut down in the maze of streets by Japanese arquebus fire, the attack was abandoned.

FURTHER READING

Black, Jeremy (ed.), *European Warfare 1453-1815* (1999)

Parker, Geoffrey, *The Military Revolution: Military Innovation and the rise of the West 1500-1800* (Cambridge, 1996)

Turnbull, Stephen, *Campaign 69: Nagashino 1575* (Oxford, 2000)

Turnbull, Stephen, *The Samurai Sourcebook* (Cassell, 1998)

Turnbull, Stephen, *Samurai Warfare* (Cassell, 1996)

ABOUT THE AUTHOR

Stephen Turnbull is the leading authority outside Japan on the military history of the samurai. His previous books for Osprey include Men-at-Arms 86: *Samurai Armies 1550-1658*, Men-at-Arms 105: *The Mongols* and, most recently, Campaign 69: *Nagashino 1575*. Stephen is currently working on a number of other book projects and can be heard lecturing on the samurai on 18 June at Leeds Paxton Horticultural Society Hall, 186 Kirkstall Lane, Leeds, 10.00am-5.30pm. Contact (0)113 258 1508.

Japanese castles and the Korean campaigns

To surround a European city with the elaborate and mathematically intricate trace italienne castles built of stone was a very expensive undertaking, so many used the same design but employed earthworks instead. As in the Japanese experience in Korea and at Osaka these were found to have the advantage of both speed and cost, and provided a deep area of absorbency for cannon shot. So far the parallels are clear, but, as noted above, we have to envisage a contemporary Japanese castle either without its tower keep, or with many other encircling walls and bastions if we are to appreciate the reality of siege warfare at the end of the Sengoku-jidai and the similarities to European artillery fortresses. This is not always easy to do in Japan, but when the Japanese invaded Korea they established a chain of coastal fortresses called *wajô* to protect their communications with Japan. As the wajô never received the tower keeps added later to Japanese castles their remains provide useful information about contemporary castle design and allow a direct comparison with European models. Instead of the Chinese and Korean styles of walls snaking up and down the mountains we see the more labour-intensive Japanese model of large scale excavations to provide horizontal surfaces, and the use of carefully designed sloping walls rather than the simpler Korean walls of flat stone. Some castles had to be built very quickly, and thousands of Japanese labourers were shipped over to help with construction work, where they joined many thousands more captive Koreans. At Ulsan even the walls and gateways were incomplete as the Ming forces advanced upon it in the winter of 1597, and an eyewitness recorded the brutality meted out by the commanders to the Korean and Japanese labourers impressed to the task. Earthworks and palisades added to the hasty defences where there was no time to build with stone, and a chronicler noted how it gave the illusion that the third bailey was complete. When the Chinese attacks began many samurai were still encamped outside the unfinished walls.

The fact that nearly all Korean castles had collapsed before the initial Japanese advance, spearheaded by volleys from massed ranks of gunners, was the main reason why the invaders spurned the native style of fortress design. One other reason why native Korean models was rejected was that a coastal location makes its own demands upon a castle designer. There was a requirement for excellent visibility, particularly out to sea, and a vital need to provide a well-defended anchorage that could in some way be linked securely to the fortress on the hill behind, where one existed. The best example of this is Sunchôn, which is very well preserved. The whole area is exactly as it was once the mountain had been scooped away and the stone facings added. As probably little else was built in the form of superstructure Sunchôn may well be one of the best preserved Japanese castle sites in the world.

When the Chinese launched their attacks on the wajô the theory held good, and the combination of gunfire covering every angle of a simple but solid series of bastions meant that the Japanese did not lose a single one of their castles. However, the overall progress of the war meant that the Japanese wajô in Korea ended up being purely defensive structures to cover the Japanese withdrawal rather than as the outposts of empire. Had things gone differently then the wajô might well have represented a parallel with the coastal forts of the Europeans, who established garrisons defended by artillery at places like Mombasa, Havana and Manila to serve as bases for overseas expansion and colonisation. Instead the samurai returned home in defeat, and put into practice the lessons they had learned from the successful repulse of the huge assaults the Chinese had mounted on their wajô. The results were to be seen in the defence systems and attacking practices used in the sieges of Otsu and Fushimi in the Sekigahara campaign of 1600, the siege of Osaka in 1615, and the overall design of many of the castles we see in Japan today. Once again it was the combination of wall and gun in the *trace japonaise* that had held them off. In Korea the lesson originally learned at Nagashino had been subjected to its most searching test and had passed with flying colours. The evolution in castle design from mountain stockade to an artillery fortress of stone was therefore complete, and owed much to the initial confirmation of the power of guns in a fortified position that was demonstrated so powerfully for the first time on the bloody field of Nagashino.

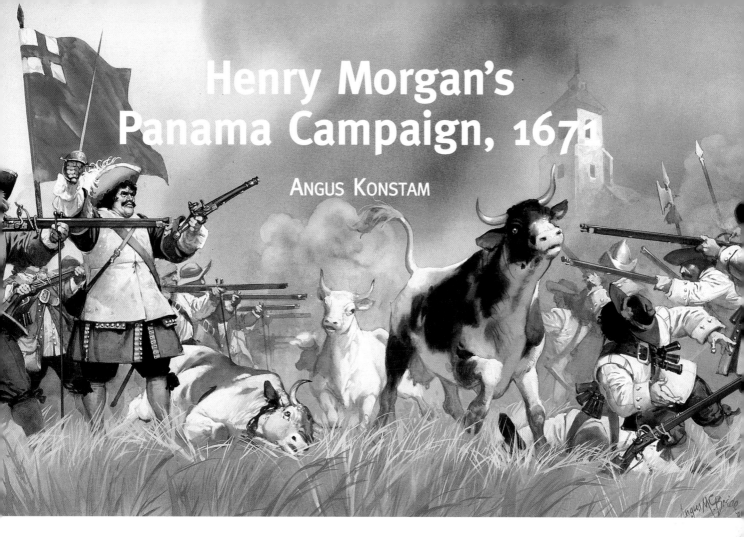

Henry Morgan's Panama Campaign, 1671

ANGUS KONSTAM

The plate shows the disciplined nature of the buccaneers' line. Although they lacked the uniformity of a regular army, they were veteran musketeers, and their volley fire was superior to anything their Spanish opponents were capable of. The Spanish city militia were issued with white uniforms, although their appearance was not as regular as that of European troops of the same period. (© 2000 Osprey Publishing Ltd. from Elite 69: Buccaneers 1620-1700 by Angus Konstam, illustration by Angus McBride)

The true test of a military commander is the way he copes with adversity. Even the most experienced leader would be challenged to retain control of mutinous troops during a forced march on starvation rations. In 1671 a Welsh pirate demonstrated his abilities by operating under exactly these conditions, his men performing feats that regular troops would have regarded as impossible.

Henry Morgan, the greatest buccaneer of them all is perhaps one of the great unsung military commanders of the 17th century. During his campaign against Panama in 1671 his men assaulted an 'impregnable' fortress, marched through some of the most in-hospitable terrain in the world, then fought and won a full-scale battle, the largest seen in the Americas until the American Revolution. Of all these achievements, his march across Panama is the least known, and deserves to be among the epic marches of history.

THE BRETHREN OF THE COAST

When the English captured Jamaica from the Spanish in 1655 they felt unable to defend the island from attack. Consequently the Governor actively encouraged 'buccaneers' to settle in Port Royal, the main harbour on the island's southern coast.

In return for official support they defended the island from attack, and by the mid-1660s buccaneers operated throughout the Caribbean basin, a region known as the 'Spanish Main'. As buccaneering raids became larger, leaders arose to command these expeditions. By 1670 Henry Morgan had become the effective leader of the Port Royal buccaneers, who called themselves 'the brethren of the coast'. In 1668 the Welshman led successful attacks on the Spanish city of Porto Bello on the isthmus of Panama and into Lake Maracaibo in Venezuela.

In late 1670 he proposed an attack on Panama, reputedly the richest Spanish city in the Americas. In August 1670, Governor Modyford gave Morgan permission to 'doe and performe all matter of exploits which may tend to the preservation and quiett of Jamaica'.

Morgan took this as official approval for his Panama scheme.

During November and December of 1670 he gathered a fleet of 26 ships and 1,200 men. These buccaneers were a unique breed – sailors who specialised in raiding the ports of the Spanish Main. Most of the force gathering in Port Royal was English, although the expedition also included French Huguenot and Dutch buccaneers, Protestant seamen united in their hatred for the Spanish. Morgan sailed on 18 December, bound for the Spanish outpost of New Providence Island. Another force of four ships and 470 men commanded by Joseph Brodely sailed for the mouth of Panama's Chagres River. This was Morgan's chosen invasion route across the Panama isthmus, but guarding the

The inside cover of the original Dutch edition of Alexandre Exquemelin's The Buccaneers of America. *The book was an instant best seller, and an English edition was published in 1684. (Author's Collection)*

river mouth was the formidable Spanish fortress of San Lorenzo.

THE ASSAULT ON SAN LORENZO

Columbus had discovered the mouth of the Chagres River in 1502, and by 1670 the river formed part of the transportation route across the isthmus from Panama to Porto Bello. Peru produced more silver than any other region in the world, and every year the treasure was shipped up the Pacific coast to Panama before being

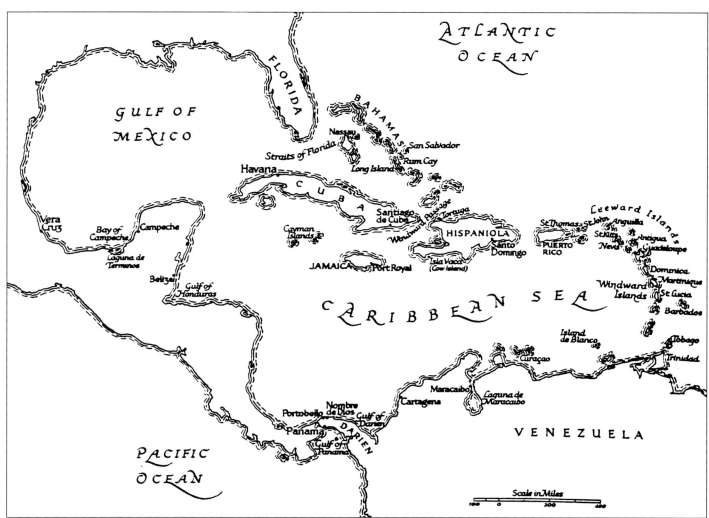

Map of the Spanish Main, c.1670. The strategic location of Jamaica in the centre of the Caribbean basin allowed the buccaneers to threaten all parts of the Spanish overseas empire, whose principal ports are shown here. (The Hensley Collection, Ashville, N. Carolina)

transported overland to Porto Bello by mule train. When river levels were high the Spaniards preferred to ship the treasure down the Chagres River for the last leg of its journey to Porto Bello, where it met the annual treasure fleet which transported it on to Spain. In 1603 a fortress called the Castillo San Lorenzo was built on top of the cliff dominating the river mouth. The summit formed a flat polygon, with steep cliffs on four sides. The final side led to a second plateau, separated from the fort by a twenty-foot deep ditch. A wooden double palisade filled with earth lined the perimeter of the plateau, and was pierced to carry 24 guns, manned by a garrison of 300 men. A six-gun battery lay at the foot of the cliff protecting the silver warehouses and the small attendant settlement.

Brodely anchored three miles from the river and approached the fortress from the east. At around 3am on 2 January the buccaneers attacked, but the garrison was ready for them, and they were repulsed with heavy losses. Brodely launched a second attack the following evening, and during the fighting a building in the fortress caught fire and the flames ignited the magazine, causing a large explosion. Brodeley's men added to the confusion by hurling grenadoes into the fort, and a section of the defences fell into the moat when a Spanish gun exploded, creating a bridge. The buccaneers swarmed into the breach, supported by covering fire. Point-blank cannon fire and musketry met them. Brodely fell in the breach, but his men swarmed on to cut down the defenders, leaving only 30 Spanish survivors. Over 100 the buccaneers were killed during the assault, or died of their wounds.

Morgan arrived a week later, losing four ships on an uncharted reef in the harbour entrance as he sailed in. Only ten men were drowned, but much of the buccaneers' provisions were lost.

An early buccaneer on Hispaniola, shown with his hunting dog and musket. These boucanniers were skilled marksmen, and by the mid-17th century had turned from hunting to piracy. (The Hensley Collection, Ashville, N. Carolina)

A **buccaneer** is the name given to pirates operating in the Caribbean during the 17th century. In theory most were 'privateers' rather than pirates, operating under licence from the English, French or Dutch colonial authorities. Whilst they were free to attack these nations' enemies during wartime, most buccaneers blurred the legal definition and caused mayhem in the Spanish Main regardless of official sanction, peace treaty or rules of warfare. Religious differences also encouraged the mainly Protestant buccaneers' hatred for the Spanish.

Henry Morgan recruiting for a raid. Drawing by Howard Pyle, for Harper's Weekly, *1885. The atmospheric work of artists such as Pyle helped to ensure that an ill-deserved romanticism surrounded the 17th-century buccaneers. (The Hensley Collection, Ashville, N. Carolina)*

It took Morgan six more days to reorganise his forces and prepare for his advance on Panama. Without adequate food, the expedition would have to live off whatever they could plunder along the way. Morgan decided the risk was worth taking.

THE MARCH TO PANAMA

On the afternoon of Sunday, 18 January 1671, Henry Morgan led his men south up the Chagres River – 1,200 men in 32 large canoes, accompanied by five small boats carrying artillery pieces. They covered less than twenty miles that day, the boats putting ashore at a small riverside hamlet, where the men could stretch their cramped limbs and sleep. Morgan had hoped to plunder supplies from the Spanish settlements he passed, but he quickly discovered that the Spanish had stripped the land of any supplies which could support his men. According to Morgan's biographer

Esquemeling (or Exquemelin), the buccaneers had nothing but tobacco to help satisfy their hunger. At dawn on the following morning the flotilla continued upriver, and by mid-afternoon had reached the hamlet of Cruz de Juan Gallego. Morgan found that the summer weather had dried the river sufficiently to bar further progress, and in any case fallen trees had created an impenetrable barrier. The buccaneers would have to abandon their boats.

The buccaneers made camp in the village, and early on 20 January Morgan began the march inland, leaving a company of 160 men to guard the canoes and artillery. Progress through the jungle was excruciatingly slow and Morgan was eventually forced to abandon the attempt. Back on the river he marched his men along its banks, towing a handful of canoes containing the muskets and powder. The

buccaneers made slow progress through the shallows, and on reaching the hamlet of Cedro Bueno he sent the canoes back to pick up more men and supplies. This gruelling process continued into the night, but eventually he had gathered all of his men in the village. It was another night of exhaustion and hunger, as no provisions could be found anywhere near the camp. At dawn the expedition continued south, while two light canoes travelled ahead of them, probing the banks for Spanish ambushes. At noon contact was made with the Spanish at the village of Torna Cavellos, and the buccaneers were heartened, hoping that the garrison would have supplies of food for the taking. When the main body arrived they found that the battalion-sized enemy force had fled, taking their provisions with them. This was a bitter disappointment, and Esquemeling reported that the men boiled and ate the leather equipment left behind by the Spaniards. In the late afternoon Morgan continued his march, reaching another settlement just behind the Spaniards, but again the buccaneers found the area stripped of all provisions. Morgan's men were now literally starving to death.

On the fifth day of the march (22 January) the buccaneers reached the village of Barbacoa, and this time the Spanish had been less thorough. In a storage cavern the English found a cache of food which had been overlooked: two sacks of meal, two vats of wine and a stack of plantains. Morgan divided the small haul amongst his men, with the majority going to those who appeared to be closest to death from starvation. It is a credit to Morgan's powers of leadership that these tough buccaneers allowed him to divide the supplies along humanitarian lines. The march continued in the late afternoon, with the worst affected men travelling in the canoes, the rest marching alongside on the bank. At nightfall Morgan camped on the site of an abandoned plantation.

At dawn on Friday 23 January Morgan's men continued along the river, reaching an abandoned plantation at midday, where they found salvation in the form of a warehouse containing maize, which Morgan divided in the same manner as before. This discovery probably did more than anything else to save the expedition, and to seal the fate of Panama. With a little food in their bellies and haversacks the buccaneers continued on, following their now established pattern of marching in the morning and late afternoon, with a rest stop around noon. That afternoon the scouts came upon a group of Indians, allies of the Spanish. The natives melted into the jungle when attacked, but a number of buccaneers were killed by arrows

Grenadoes were basic 17th-century grenades: hollow iron spheres filled with gunpowder and projectiles such as musket shot or scraps of metal. A wooden fuse was fitted into a hole in the sphere and a short length of slow match inserted inside it. Timing was inaccurate, but once lit a grenade would explode in less than a minute. Some buccaneers and pirates even used spirit bottles rather than metal spheres, making them a forerunner of the Molotov Cocktail.

A European soldier of the 1670s preparing a grenade for throwing. From Allain Mallet's Les Travaux de Mars (Paris, 1672). Buccaneers frequently used grenades when storming Spanish fortifications. (National Army Musuem, London)

during the skirmish. The Indian ambush was laid at a river crossing and hamlet called Santa Cruz, important only in that it marked the point where the river curved to the east. Morgan crossed the river and pitched camp for the night on the southern bank. Esquemeling reports that during the evening many buccaneers complained about their predicament, but elected to continue rather than return empty-handed. They were now close to Venta de Cruces, a town astride the road from Panama to Porto Bello, and the terminus used when silver was shipped downstream to San Lorenzo. Morgan expected the town to be strongly defended, and indeed the Governor of Panama, Juan Peréz de Guzmán was there in person at the head of 800 militia and his Indian auxiliaries. He had ordered the 'scorched earth' policy that was

proving so effective, and assured his men that the buccaneers were a starving rabble. His men remained unconvinced, and when the majority deserted during the night he had little option but to withdraw, leaving a rearguard to harass the invaders.

On the morning of 24 January Morgan made his men clean their firearms, and prepare themselves for battle. At noon they saw smoke rising above the trees as they approached the village from the west. The buccaneers hoped the smoke came from cooking fires, but when they entered the village they found it came from burning buildings. The Spanish had abandoned the town in accordance with their 'scorched earth' policy, destroying everything except the government warehouses and stables. These substantial buildings formed a staging post for the annual mule trains which carried silver from Panama to the Caribbean coast, but they were found to be empty apart from wine jars and a sack of bread. This feast was consumed in minutes, and the

buccaneers spent the rest of the day searching the ruins for scraps of food, which included shooting any stray dog or cat they found. Some of the buccaneers roved outside the town, where they were attacked by Spanish soldiers, and one man was captured. To protect his men Morgan ordered that nobody was to leave the town perimeter unless as part of a company-sized unit. With his force in such bad condition, and so deep in enemy territory, he could ill afford to lose men in minor skirmishes, but intermittent firing continued throughout the day.

Morgan spent the night camped in the town ready for a Spanish attack which never came. The next morning he led his men south along the trail leading to Panama (known as the Camino de Cruces). San Lorenzo lay 70 miles behind them, while their objective was now only 24 miles ahead, along a firm road. The canoes were sent back to rejoin the rest of his river flotilla, leaving one canoe as a messenger boat. His small army was

The battle of Panama 1671, a scene which includes many of the features of the conflict, in no particular order. Of note are the stampeding cattle in the centre, and a buccaneer musket body repulsing Spanish cavalry in the right corner. from Exquemelin, 1684. (Author's Collection)

then divided into two main divisions, each of 400 men, preceded by an advanced guard of 200 men. This vanguard contained the best of Morgan's marksmen, and it was commanded by the highly experienced Dutch buccaneer Laurens Prins. This deployment was vital given the terrain: a region of hills, passes and woodland which extended for almost 15 miles before the hilly inland plateau gave way to the flatter coastal plain. All went well for several hours until the vanguard reached a defile, where they were suddenly showered by Indian arrows loosed by a hidden enemy. Although their assailants fled and no men were killed, Prins remained cautious, and beyond the pass his scouts located the Indians gathered in a wood. Most fled, but a small group of Indians stood their ground and fought the buccaneers. The defenders broke when their chief was killed by a pistol shot, but the skirmish cost the lives of eight buccaneers, with a further ten wounded. Prins sent 50 scouts ahead of the vanguard, who reported that the Indians were attached to a larger Spanish force. Prins took up a position on high ground beside the trail and called for Morgan and his main force. After a tense delay it was found that the Spaniards had withdrawn back towards Panama, and the march continued. As dusk fell a heavy tropical downpour broke and Morgan's men sought shelter in a small village. There were not enough buildings to shelter more than a fraction of his men, so Morgan ordered that the buildings be reserved for weapons and powder, and the buccaneers including Morgan spent a miserable and hungry night exposed to the elements.

Dawn broke on Monday 26 January to find Morgan already marching south under overcast skies. During the early morning they were shadowed by Spanish scouts, who kept the invaders

Henry Morgan shown standing before the city of Panama in 1671. The well-dressed buccaneer commander is shown carrying a flintlock musket, indicating how readily the buccaneers embraced a weapon that was technically far superior to the matchlock musket. (The Hensley Collection, Ashville, N. Carolina)

under observation from a distance, and shortly after 9am the buccaneers reached the crest of Culebra, the last hill of the inland plateau. It presented the buccaneers with a view of 'that desired place, the Southern Sea', or Pacific Ocean. If Morgan felt any foreboding when he saw a treasure galleon sailing south from Panama, he kept his thoughts to himself. Another more welcome sight lay closer at hand. Morgan's scouts found a large herd of cattle, which were promptly rounded up and killed. It is probable that these were some of the animals which the Indian auxiliaries had driven from the plantations along the Chagres River. Fires were started, the cattle were butchered and Morgan's men gorged themselves on the first real food they had tasted since leaving San Lorenzo

nine days before. Esquemeling claimed that 'they devoured them with incredible taste and appetite. Such was their hunger that they more resembled cannibals than Europeans at this banquet'. The march was resumed in the afternoon, but this time the buccaneers had as much food as they could carry, and their objective was within reach. Spanish cavalry circled just out of range, yelling insults at the buccaneers, including 'cornudos' (cuckolds) and 'perros Ingleses' (English dogs). The buccaneers ignored them, and by late afternoon they sighted Panama through the trees. The buccaneers made camp behind a slight rise about a mile north of the city, and it was clear to everyone that battle was imminent.

During the evening Spanish artillery on the city walls fired an ineffectual bombardment at the buccaneer camp. A Spanish company also blocked the trail behind the buccaneers, effectively preventing them from retreating without a fight. Both these actions failed to alarm Morgan's men, who lit fires and cooked their evening meal. During the night Morgan's scouts had probed the approaches to the city, and revealed that a frontal attack was too dangerous. An approach along the axis of Camino las Cruces would be subject to fire from artillery placed on the walls and by flanking fire from outlying earthworks. A newly-built redoubt dominated the approach, containing even more artillery and a small garrison. Morgan therefore laid plans for an indirect approach march, using the woods to the west of his camp as cover.

THE BATTLE BEFORE PANAMA

On the morning of 27 January Morgan formed up his men 'with drums and trumpets sounding' and began marching towards the city. His intention was evidently to divert the enemy, as he soon moved his men off the road to the right into the woods. The Spanish and the buccaneers lost contact with each other for a short while until Morgan's men reappeared on a small rise a mile or so to the west. The Spanish governor was left with no alternative but to face the buccaneers in the open field, as he was unable to redeploy enough of his artillery to adequately protect the western side of the city. Therefore in the mid morning the two small armies faced each other, separated by two miles of boggy open ground. A slight rise or 'hammock' dominated the open plain to the east of the battlefield, immediately to the front right of the Spanish line.

The Spanish were formed in line with their foot in the centre and their flanks protected by cavalry. The infantry were all militia, formed into four regiments, each of approximately six companies of around 50 men each. The formations were arrayed six deep in the current Spanish style, with the musketeers protected by pikemen (a musket: pike ratio of 2:1 was probable). The 400 militia cavalry were split into two squadrons, one on each wing. The Spaniards also had a trick up their sleeves, as they had rounded up a herd of several hundred cattle, which the governor planned to stampede into the buccaneer ranks at a critical moment. Governor Peréz de Guzmán commanded his troops in person, assisted by the Alcalde (mayor) of Panama, and an un-named Spanish army colonel, a military attaché to the Governor's staff. It is unclear whether he included field artillery in his line of battle. Artillery was readily available, but if used its part in the battle was not commented on by the participants.

Morgan dressed his men, who were organised into the three divisions which had been formed at Las Cruces. The buccaneers then advanced; 'their red and green banners clearly visible to the Spaniards … [who] were posted in a spacious field waiting for their coming'. Prins was on the left wing with his vanguard, Morgan remained in the centre with the main body, while another commander, probably Robert Searle, commanded the rearguard. Each main division contained less than 400 men, while the vanguard was formed from the remains of Prins' 200 picked men. As Esquemeling reports:

As soon as they drew nigh unto them, the Spaniards began to shout, and cry 'Viva el Rey' [Long Live the King], and immediately their horse began to move against the pirates.

This appeared to be an impromptu charge of the cavalry on the Spanish right wing, launched against Prins' division. The boggy ground slowed down the Spanish, and Prins was able to receive them in line with an organised volley from his buccaneers formed into three ranks:

Every one putting a knee to the ground, gave them a full volley of shot, wherewith the battle was instantly kindled very hot.

With half the horsemen killed or wounded, the remainder withdrew, a similar but less determined charge on the buccaneer's right flank was also repulsed. Musketeers detached from the foot units 'endeavoured to second the horse, but were constrained by the pirates to separate from them'. In other words, concentrated volley fire had pinned down the two wings of the Spanish army.

Peréz de Guzmán decided to launch his secret weapon, and called for the cattle to be released. The drovers promptly fled, and the cattle ran aimlessly between or through the two armies, or stampeded from the field. Driven frantic by the gunfire, the animals proved to be more of a hindrance for the Spaniards than for the buccaneers. As Esquemeling observed:

Some few that broke through the English companies did no other harm than to tear the colours into pieces, whereas the buccaneers, shooting them dead, left not one to trouble them thereabouts.

By this time the Spanish militia infantry had seen their cavalry wings dissolve, and their own ranks disrupted by stampeding cattle. As a last resort the Governor ordered them to advance on the buccaneers. They were met by a withering fire, and the advance stalled. They stood their ground for a few minutes and tried to exchange fire within 50 yards of the buccaneer line, but they were no match for the buccaneers

… which being perceived by the foot, and that they could not possibly prevail, they discharged the shot they had in their muskets, and throwing them on

the ground, betook themselves to flight, every one which way he could run.

The poorly trained Spanish militia armed with matchlock muskets proved no match for Morgan's veterans armed almost exclusively with flintlocks. Peréz de Guzmán's attempts to rally his men were fruitless, and he fled towards the city, where a boat waited to take him to safety.

Many of the rest of the Spanish soldiers were not so lucky. The buccaneers offered them no quarter, and even a group of clergymen who came out to beg Morgan to spare the city were cut down, at least according to Esquemeling. It still might have been possible to stop the buccaneers entering the city, but the fleeing Spanish troops pouring through the gates prevented their closure. The buccaneers followed on behind, and although some Spanish gunners remained at their posts and fired at the attackers (probably mowing down some of their own routed troops), they were unable to prevent them entering the city. The buccaneers slaughtered anyone who dared to oppose them, and the Spanish inhabitants fled for the eastern gate and for the harbour, where they escaped in anything that would float. The chaos must have been indescribable, but by noon, Morgan had established complete control of the city.

THE AFTERMATH

Panama proved to be a less than lucrative prize. All of the royal treasure had been removed in the galleon spotted by Morgan from the plateau, and most of the city's private wealth had also been removed before the buccaneers arrived. The richest Spanish prize in the Americas proved to contain little for Morgan's men to plunder. The buccaneers remained in the city for several more weeks, searching the hinterland for hidden plunder, torturing any Spaniards they

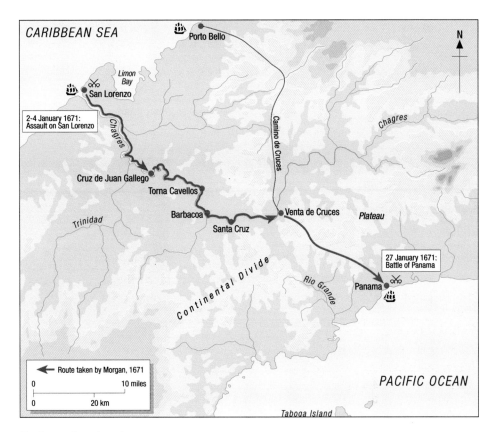

The Panama Campaign, 1671

found to reveal the location of secret caches of valuables. By February the buccaneers felt that they had extorted all they could from the region and retraced their steps to San Lorenzo and their ships. The mood of the buccaneers was volatile, as the average haul had come to less than £18 sterling per man (totalling roughly £50,000/$80,000 today), a fraction of the plunder taken at Porto Bello. Many accused Morgan of cheating them, so he quickly ordered his men to disband and sailed for Port Royal in mid-May, 1671. On his arrival he found that while he was away, Spain and England had made peace, which made his actions legally questionable, and any further attacks unacceptable. Before the end of the year he was taken to England to answer charges levelled by the Crown (at the insistence of the Spanish ambassador). Morgan was eventaully acquitted, and, to the chagrin of the Spanish ambassador, he was even appointed as

the new Deputy Governor of Jamaica. He died in Jamaica in 1688 at the age of 53, his demise reputedly hastened by excessive drinking. The Panama campaign was Morgan's last raid, and marked the end of the English buccaneering era in the Spanish Main. What remains is the legacy of his achievements. He marched a make-shift army of lawless pirates over 100 miles through the jungles, swamps and infested rivers of Central America to take his private war into the very heart of the Spanish overseas empire. Although renowned as a great pirate chief, his exploits would stand alongside those of other more celebrated military commanders.

Note: Much of the route used by Morgan lies beneath the Panama Canal, which follows the Chagres River for much of its course. Panama was abandoned after Morgan sacked the city, and a new city built eight miles down the coast. The ruins of old Panama and San Lorenzo are now historic attractions.

SUGGESTED READING

Cruickshank, E. A., *The Life of Sir Henry Morgan*, (Toronto, 1935)

Earle, Peter, *The Sack of Panama: Henry Morgan's Adventures on the Spanish Main,* (New York, 1981)

Esquemeling, John, *The Buccaneers of America*, (London, 1685)

Marley, David H., *Pirates: Adventurers on the High Seas*, (London, 1995)

Parry, J. H., *The Spanish Seaborne Empire*, (London, 1966)

Pope, Dudley, *Harry Morgan's Way: The Biography of Sir Henry Morgan 1635-1684*, (London, 1977)

ABOUT THE AUTHOR

Angus Konstam has written a number of books for Osprey, mainly on 18th century subjects. His recent works include Campaign 44: *Pavia 1525* and Elite 67: *Pirates 1670-1730*. Angus previously worked as a curator of weapons at the Royal Armouries, London, and Chief Curator of the Mel Fisher Maritime Museum, Florida. His most recent work is Elite 69: *Buccaneers 1600-1700*, due for publication in June 2000 **(see Messenger pages for a Men-at-Arms special offer in conjunction with this forthcoming publication)**.

Conte Collectibles: PIRATES!

The new Pirates figure and collectible set from Conte Collectibles (2037 Grouse St., Las Vegas, NV 89134, T (702) 233-8201 F (702) 233-8206) is tremendous. The thirty-one 54mm figures and 54mm pirate ship are in scale and the figures come in poses which should satisfy every collector. This new 54mm series contains pirates, buccaneers, and the scum of every seaport in the Caribbean. Unlike many scale figure releases, this has one important item most sets don't – a 54mm pirate sloop in scale, three feet in length, moulded with exquisite detail and just begging to go on a bookshelf. The yard-long pirate vessel sports two rows of guns on naval carriages, and comes complete with rogues in every pose expected, including brawlers, buccaneers with boat hooks and grappling irons, cutlasses, blunderbusses, muskets, a lookout in the crow's nest, and a pirate captain modelled on Blackbeard the Pirate (Edward Teach). Blackbeard is posed with a snarl on his face, cutlass in one hand, dagger in the other, and a brace of pistols in his belt. His beard is curled and separated by ribbons, and he has the most fearsome expression of glee since Robert Newton brought the character to film. A uniformed naval officer, Lt. Maynard, opposes the pirates and points a pistol at his enemies while brandishing a cutlass. There is a comely female pirate dressed in a jerkin and hip boots firing one pistol with another held ready and wearing a cutlass in her belt. Another rogue carries off a screaming wench slung over his shoulder, and a six-man gun crew mans a naval gun with ruthless efficiency (only five are shown in the picture). An unfortunate stands ready to walk the plank (something more common in fiction than actual practice), a pair of swordsmen parry and slash, and another pirate swings from the rigging (whereas the Royal Navy would like him to swing from a yardarm). There is even a partial skeleton of a decomposed pirate lying in the sand. These 54mm collector figures are moulded in tan plastic, come unpainted and posed every way imaginable, and bring to life the Jolly Roger and the days of adventure on the high seas. Great attention has been paid to accuracy of weaponry and costume, and all figures are well posed so they will bring a diorama to life. This is a good complement to earlier Conte releases such as The War Lord, Zulu, Spartacus, Beau Geste, and The Longest Day licensed historical figures and playsets for the movies, and if anything their high quality improves with each new release. The figures are well-sculpted and highly animated, capturing the feel of this swashbuckling era for the collector and gamer.

Carl Smith

LANDMARKS IN HISTORY

For over 2000 years the Tower of London has been one of the focal points of the city, and is now one of the most famous and visited landmarks in the world. To coincide with a major exhibition to celebrate this wealth of history, Osprey has collaborated with the Royal Armouries to produce a new history of the Tower from its earliest days.

The history of the Tower of London began long before William of Normandy constructed the famous White Tower in the 11th century as a symbol of his power as Conqueror. The land has been an important tactical site since pre-Roman times, and its history has always been turbulent and bloody. To bring the past 2000 years of the Tower dramatically to life, 14 specially commissioned artworks depict a 'snapshot' view of the Tower at different points in its history, providing a unique visual chronicle of its changing landscapes and buildings through the ages. Geoffrey Parnell, the Royal Armouries official Keeper of Tower History, reveals the changing life of the Tower in a compelling and exciting narrative.

See *The Messenger* (page 60) to find out how to order this title.

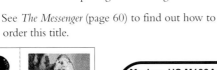

LANDMARKS IN HISTORY
THE TOWER OF LONDON
A 2000-YEAR HISTORY

IVAN LAPPER
GEOFFREY PARNELL

OSPREY

French soldiers preparing chicken and beef for the troops. (Print after Martinet)

Chicken Marengo –
A Gastronomic Re-enactment

René Chartrand

French infantry grenadier of the Revolutionary wars. Note the fine chicken tied to his knapsack. (Print after Seele)

The story of this delicious dish, so closely associated with Napoleon, can be found in countless recipe books, especially from the later part of the 19th century, and in French or English. Immediately after the battle of Marengo General Bonaparte's chef, Dunand, had a serious problem. The French army's supplies were still a considerable distance to the rear and Napoleon, who was quite hungry, wanted his dinner now. There was no arguing about such basic matters with the General and Dunand knew he simply had to make do with what few things he had immediately to hand. That would be the victory dinner.

The only ingredients available were a small chicken, eggs, some crayfish écrevisse, truffles and tomatoes, garlic and olive oil. Soon, Dunand was busy frying all this up and it proved to be one of the most delicious dishes Napoleon had ever tasted. Word soon got around and everybody tried it, and was equally delighted. Gastronomic history had been made … or had it?

First, the idea of a celebration dinner does not fit well with what is known of Napoleon's mood following the battle. It was a brilliant victory but one of his best friends, General Desaix, had been killed. First-hand accounts, such as those of Captain Gervais or Sergeant Coignet, tell of shortage of food but nothing more specific. Napoleon's personal valet, Constant, certainly one of the men who would have been closest to him at this specific time, does not mention any kind of dinner for Napoleon that night. He 'slept on the battlefield', Constant noted, and 'in spite of the decisive victory he had just won, he was full of grief, and, in the evening, said many things to Hambart [the head valet] and myself which proved the profound affliction that he felt at the lost of General Desaix.' Nearby were Desaix's ADC's, Rapp and Savary, 'plunged in a bitter despair' as they grieved by the body of their dead chief who had been like a father to them. It was hardly the atmosphere for a victory dinner at Napoleon's HQ that night.

For all that, 'Chicken Marengo' did exist. Bourrienne, Napoleon's secretary, tells us about it in his recollections of the First Consul's eating habits.

At ten every morning, luncheon was served for Napoleon and his entourage, cooked in oil and onions, a modest dish which was named, I think, chicken à la Provencale, and it has since been perpetuated on the menus of our restaurants in memory of a famous battle with the more ambitious name of chicken à la Marengo.

Constant also noted that:

the Emperor's favourite dish was a sort of chicken fricassée – which, due to the preference of the winner of Italy, was given the name of Chicken Marengo.

Thus, it seems fairly certain that Dunand, the 'inventor' of the recipe, must have been cooking this dish long before the battle that gave it its name. It only became famous when restaurants started offering it as a result of the 'Napoleonmania' which swept Paris following the victory.

The news of the victory at Marengo was received with tremendous joy in Paris and, when Napoleon came back, he was mobbed and hailed by great crowds everywhere. People wanted to know everything about their idol and it must have been then that his favourite, simple Provencale dish was renamed Marengo.

The renown of the dish swept France and Europe and crossed the oceans. In 1819, the Montreal butcher Boyer advertised chickens suitable for making Chicken Marengo, by then clearly a well-known recipe in North America.

The early recipe given here is at variance with versions seen in later cookbooks and attributed to Dunand. Tomato is an especially 'suspect' ingredient. Tomatoes were not commonly used in cooking at that time and are hardly ever mentioned in cookbooks until the second half of the 19th century. Freshwater crayfish was used in various dishes in 18th and 19th century French cuisine, then disappeared gradually. However, it is very

This recipe is an elaboration of the original basic dish as it would have been prepared in the years immediately after the battle.

To re-enact Napoleon's early lunch or dinner on 14 June 1800, if he had any, omit all ingredients except the chicken, onion, garlic and oil, and perhaps add some dried herbs.

It will serve four, preparation and cooking time about an hour.

INGREDIENTS

One medium chicken
(preferably free range)

Half a cup of olive oil

Mushrooms
(preferably field or forest, not little white buttons),

Bouquet garni
(fresh Italian flat parsley, preferably, bay leaf, thyme and 3 of the mushrooms, finely chopped green onion tied in a bunch),

Eggs and bread to garnish, optional

For the sauce:
Butter
Two tablespoons chopped parsley
Chopped shallot or small onion
Three of the mushrooms finely chopped
Glass of white wine

- Cut up the chicken into six pieces.

  Sprinkle with salt and fry gently in the oil for about 45 minutes in a large pan over a moderate heat. If preferred, brown the chicken first in a little of the oil over a higher heat.

- While the chicken is leisurely frying, make the wine sauce by melting the butter in a small pan, enough to cover the base genrously, adding the garlic, shallot, parsley and the three chopped mushrooms.

- Cook at medium heat for just a few minutes, shaking the pan occasionally, then add the wine.

- Lower to a gentle simmer, cover and leave for about 20 minutes.

- When the chicken has been cooking for about 30 minutes, add the rest of the mushrooms, a double handful roughly chopped, and the bouquet garni. If you are in the money, you could now also add a finely sliced truffle for a delicious flavour of Northern Italy; some early recipes mention this.

- When done, arrange the chicken pieces and mushroom on a serving dish.

- Remove the bouquet garni and mix the cooking juices into the sauce then pour over the chicken.

- To finish off the dish in period style, arrange fried eggs and croutons (buttered bread toasted or fried) around the chicken.

unlikely to have been available at Marengo in an army that had just crossed the Alps by the St Bernard Pass. Truffles are found in Piedmont but, again, seem unlikely in the circumstances. It was in the latter part of the 19th century that Chicken Marengo became such a luxurious affair with truffles and crayfish. Auguste Escoffier, who was then France's most famous chef, author of the famous 1902 *Guide Culinaire* and a favourite of Edward VII, has Chicken Marengo cooking in olive oil. But for the sauce and dressing, we now have to do the following:

Take out the chicken pieces once they are cooked and empty the oil out of the frying pan. Add a glass of white wine and let simmer on the fire until reduced by half, then add two peeled and diced tomatoes, two tablespoons of tomato paste, a crushed garlic clove, ten small mushrooms already cooked, ten slices of truffle and half a cup of veal broth, and stir everything together. Once it is piping hot, pour over the chicken pieces and decorate with four cooked crayfish.

To the joy of restaurant owners and chefs, truffles and crayfish handsomely raised the price they could charge for what had been a delicious but quite humble chicken dish, now glorified to imperial status thanks to Napoleon's great victory. Napoleon was not actually a fan of haute cuisine, preferring tasty but plain dishes that could be consumed very quickly. His eating habits were, in fact, the despair of many of his high ranking officials who delighted in exquisite gourmet cuisine in dinners that lasted three or four hours. 'The Emperor ate very fast', Constant related, 'staying only about 12 minutes at the table' if there were guests, after which he would get up and leave. He generally dined alone with Josephine and would only have one course and a modest dessert. She made sure he had his half-cup of coffee after the meal, as he would often forget it, his fertile mind always preoccupied with a multitude of things. Most often, 'the Emperor lunched alone' eating from a tray without a napkin. 'This meal, even shorter than the other, would last ten minutes.' Indeed, this habit of eating very fast, not surprisingly,

News of the victory at Marengo caused a frenzy of celebrations in Paris with Napoleon being idolized. Even his coachmen were treated by their Paris colleagues as shown in this print. It is probably from that time that Provence chicken was transformed into the glorious-sounding Chicken Marengo.

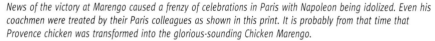

Napoleon on campaign was more interested in the camp cooking of his men than his own food. He would roam the camps to look in the pots, a practice that led to some amusing incidents when the men did not recognize him at first. (Print after JOB)

occasionally gave him stomach pains.

What would Napoleon have drunk with his favourite dish? Constant tells us red wine, nearly always cut with water, adding that the Emperor was not fond of wine, did not know vintages very well and nearly always drank Chambertin – Chambertin, one of the great wines of Burgundy, cut with water. That must have been agony for one of his generals, Marshal Angereau, a connoisseur of wine. Certainly the luxury crayfish and truffles version of Chicken Marengo, eaten with Chambertin without the added water, would make a most memorable dinner, and Gevrey-Chambertin would do well enough. For the ordinary version of Chicken Marengo that Napoleon would have eaten, ordinary red Burgundy will suffice, especially if you are going to cut it with water in the interests of research. Beaujolais also goes well with the dish. If you prefer white wine, try it with a dry, preferably French, Chardonnay.

Santé, vive l'Empereur!

SUGGESTED READING

Enjoy this dish whilst reading Camppaign 70: *Marengo 1800* by David Hollins (Osprey, available May 2000.

ABOUT THE AUTHOR

René Chartrand is a military historian and film consultant. He has written many books with Osprey, and after researching in Britain and Portugal, is currently finishing three Men-at-Arms volumes on the Portuguese Army of the Napoleonic Wars.

Napoleon's bivouac at Marengo was probably not too different that the one at Austerlitz pictured here. Note at the upper left the small figures of a grenadier chasing a chicken which, if caught, will soon be the principal ingredient in Napoleon's favourite dish. (Print after Martinet)

OSPREY MILITARY JOURNAL

COMING SOON!

THE INTERNATIONAL REVIEW OF MILITARY HISTORY

Every two months, each richly illustrated 64 page issue will bring you a wealth of great features, pictures, maps and charts, historic sites to visit, and reviews of new books, games, models and miniatures. Here are just a few of the articles you can look forward to enjoying soon:

ISSUE 2.4

This Issue will span nineteen centuries from 43 AD to 1942 covering the battlefields of England, France, North America and the Mediterranean.

- **Neil Grant** investigates the rival claims of Sussex and Kent to the beacheads for the Emperor Claudius's legions, reviewing archaeological and historical evidence and the political, strategic and tactical arguments on either side.

- Moving to northern France and the battle of **Crécy** in 1346, **Dr David Nicolle** explains the failure of the French to make effective use of their **elite Genoese crossbowmen** against the English longbowmen, men-at-arms and cavalry.

- Two centuries on in 1513 much the same English tactics proved their worth for the last time, against the new European method of fighting, **bow and bill against pike**, a revival of the main infantry tactic of Philip of Macedon and Alexander the Great. **John Barratt** describes this bloody clash between England and Scotland and generations of warfare at **Flodden** in Northumberland in the English Borders country.

- Two centuries from the beginning of his extraordinary journey from Marengo to Waterloo it is a good time to re-examine Napoleon's formative earlier years. In the first of two articles **René Chartrand** looks at his military education as **Gentleman Cadet Bonaparte 1779-1785.**

- On a different continent in July 1873 the American Civil War reached its turning point at Gettysburg. **General Greene's defence of Culp's Hill** and the Union right flank between the second and third day was one of the most critical actions of the battle. **Carl Smith** tells how inspired leadership and tactics, and heroic fighting held off numerically far superior Confederate forces.

- The Mediterranean in World War II is the setting for the final article. **Anthony Rogers** describes the epic **defence of Malta** focusing on the fluctuating battle for dominance between the Royal Air Force and Royal Naval Air Service, Italy's Regia Aeronautica and the Luftwaffe and the significance of other Axis strategic priorities in the ultimate survival of this fortress island as a key Allied strongpoint in the Mediterranean and North African theatres from 1940 to 1942.

- **PLUS** book and video reviews, information on coming events, notes on models and games, and full information on new Osprey publications with readers offers and previews .

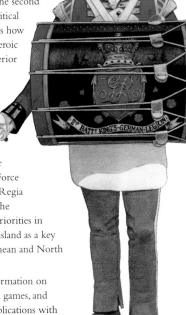

Subscribe now using the card in this issue. *Volume 2 Issue 4 available in July 2000!*

THE MESSENGER

MAY & JUNE HIGHLIGHTS

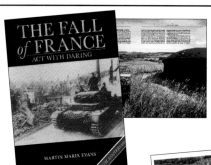

THE FALL OF FRANCE - ACT WITH DARING

Relives the unsettled summer of 1940, when Hitler's resolve to 'act with daring' took Europe by storm, and victory seemed within his grasp.

160pp • May
• £19.99 / $29.95

ENCYCLOPEDIA OF RUSSIAN AIRCRAFT

New in paperback and featuring some 1000 aircraft types, this truly is 'the' definitive work on Russian aircraft. No book in the history of aviation has ever contained so much new information.

560pp • May • £30.00 / $49.99

LANDMARKS IN HISTORY: THE TOWER OF LONDON - A 2000 YEAR HISTORY

2000 years of power struggle and bloodshed brought vividly to life in a unique pictorial chronicle of the Tower of London.

48pp • May • £4.99 / $8.95

CAMPAIGN 70: MARENGO 1800

Shedding an entirely new light on the events of Marengo, this 112pp Campaign special investigates one of the greatest 'what ifs' of military history.

112pp • May
• £11.99 / $19.95

CAMPAIGN 71: CRÉCY 1346

The tale of how the 'Black Prince' won his spurs, in a battle which established the longbow as one of the most feared weapons of its time.

96pp • June
• £10.99 / $17.95

CAMPAIGN 67: SARATOGA 1777

The battle which marked the turning point of the American War of Independence when General Burgoyne's 11,000 men surrendered in the Hudson Valley.

96pp • June
• £10.99 / $17.95

ELITE 69: BUCCANEERS 1620–1700

The period between 1620 and 1690 was a bloodthirsty time in the Caribbean, as piratical Buccaneers ravaged the islands in the names of their European monarchs.

64pp • June
• £8.99 / $14.95

New titles in the Order of Battle series

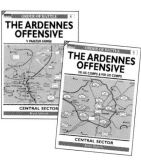

FLAGS OF THE THIRD REICH

Investigates the potent symbols and images of the Third Reich which terrorised the world from 1936 to 1945.

144pp • May
• £14.99 / $24.95

FLAGS OF THE CIVIL WAR

The flags that embodied the very essence of the different regiments that fought in the American Civil War.

144pp • May
• £14.99 / $24.95

SUPERCARRIERS: NAVAL AVIATION IN ACTION

Life 'up on the roof' of the modern aircraft carrier, with action footage of naval vessels.

144pp • June
• £16.99 / $24.95

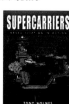

AVIATION PIONEERS 3: GERMAN AND AUSTRIAN AVIATION OF WW1

Analyses and illustrates every German and Austrian aircraft type flown in the War, detailing famous aces.

96pp • June
• £9.99 / $15.95

FRONTLINE COLOUR 3: F-84 THUNDERJET UNITS OVER KOREA

Built as a fighter, the colourful F-84 Thunderjet arrived in Korea in late 1950 and saw most of its wartime action in the bomber role.

128pp • June
• £13.99 / $19.95

BARBARIANS AGAINST ROME

Fighting engulfed proto-historic Europe, as Rome's territorial ambitions grew and Celts, Gauls and Teutones strove to retain their age-old home-lands and cultural identities.

144pp • June
• £14.99 / $24.95

ORDER OF BATTLE 8: THE ARDENNES OFFENSIVE V PANZER ARMEE CENTRAL SECTOR

ORDER OF BATTLE 9: THE ARDENNES OFFENSIVE VII US CORPS AND VIII US CORPS CENTRAL SECTOR

The second pair of volumes in the Ardennes series, detailing the action in the key central sector of the front from the Allied and then the Axis perspective.

96pp • July • £12.99 / $21.95

QUALITY ACCURACY DETAIL – NEW FROM OSPREY MODELLING MANUALS

MODELLING MANUAL 11: SOFT SKINNED MILITARY VEHICLES

How to model the range of unarmed military vehicles which are essential to so many dioramas.

64pp • June • £12.95 / $17.95

MODELLING MANUAL 12: POSTWAR AIRCRAFT

Modelling military jets from the Korean War to the present day, with particular attention to accurate detailing, marking and camouflage schemes.

64pp • June • £12.95 / $17.95

AVAILABLE THROUGH OSPREY DIRECT (SEE OPPOSITE) OR THROUGH GOOD BOOK AND HOBBY STORES

VISIT OUR NEW WEBSITE! www.ospreypublishing.com

NEWS FROM OSPREY PUBLISHING

BRINGING HISTORY TO LIFE

Selected titles from Osprey's famous Campaign, Warrior and Elite series are now available with striking new covers. All of these Classic Illustrated History editions are complete with indices and glossaries, whilst other additional features include site locator maps and visitor information. May and June releases are featured below. For details of other titles available please contact Osprey Direct or your usual supplier.

FREDERICKSBURG 1862
96pp • May • £10.99 / $17.95

SHILOH 1862 – with added visitor information
100pp • May • £11.99 / $18.95

FIRST MANASSAS 1861 – with added visitor information
100pp • May • £11.99 / $18.95

VICKSBURG 1863 – with added visitor information
100pp • May • £11.99 / $18.95

THE WARRIOR PHARAOH
96pp • June • £10.99 / $17.95

THE CHARGE OF THE LIGHT BRIGADE
96pp • June • £10.99 / $17.95

BUCCANEERS
64pp • June • £8.99 / $14.95

THE KOREAN WAR
48pp • June • £7.99 / $12.95

SARATOGA 1777
– with added visitor information
100pp • June • £11.99 / $18.95

ANTIETAM 1862 – with added visitor information
100pp • June • £11.99 / $18.95

BOSTON 1775 – with added visitor information
100pp • June • £11.99 / $18.95

Book Reviews

The White
Tecumseh
Stanley P. Hirshson
(John R. Wiley &
Sons, 605 Third
Ave., New York,
NY 10158-0012,
Tel (202) 850-6000,
$16.95)

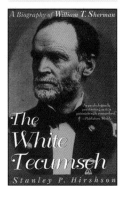

Although dealing with Sherman's entire life, Hirshson's book focuses primarily on his Civil War years. As a young officer in Louisiana, rather than sign over weapons at the Federal government arsenal from Federal to State control, he resigned from the service, only to rejoin months later as an officer in the 13th US Infantry when war was declared. From a humble rank he rapidly rose through merit in the Union army, eventually assuming command of the western theater of the war. He accomplished many things, but he is best remembered for his march to the sea, an act which bisected the South and made it clear even to diehards that the Confederate cause was doomed. 'Cump' Sherman advocated a policy of total war to bring the war to as early an end as possible, and although his campaign destroyed many plantations and towns, this march knocked the supports from underneath the sagging mansion of Southern government and ended the war earlier than if he had not been so ruthless. By making the war affect civilians, he weakened the resolve of the Confederate soldiers and weakened the Confederate infrastructure, further straining the almost non-existent supplies. Hirshson's book draws on archival records, unit histories, diaries, and military history to unfold the story of a brilliant, fiery leader with deep fears of family mental illness that he fought his entire life. Beyond the Civil War, Sherman excelled, even taking Grant to task when he thought him wrong. After the war, he became commander in chief of the army in 1869, established the army's command school at Ft. Levenworth, Kansas, and retired in 1884. Together with Sheridan, he made his mark irrevocably on the United States Army and established cavalry as the branch of service responsible for the protection of American interests in the 'wild west.' He died in 1896, and as a show of respect, one of his Confederate adversaries, Joseph E. Johnston headed his funeral cortege. Cump Sherman was an enigma, a man who fought his own demons and the enemies of his country while trying to improve the army in which he served, Hirshson's biography is a fascinating read about the convoluted life of a brilliant general.
Carl Smith

Life on Commando
During The
Anglo-Boer War
1899-1902
Fransjohan Pretorius
Translated by
Marcelle Manley,
Human &
Rousseau, 1999,
ISBN 0 7981 3808 4,
SA Rand 120

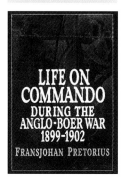

The popular image of the Boer on Commando is rather like the Hollywood portrayal of the wild west, and there is a proportion of truth in that idea. Until now, however, we who speak only English have had to make do with a few classic narratives from such writers as Christiaan de Wet and Deneys Reitz to gather a personal picture of the guerrilla fighters and their experience. In *Life on Commando during the Anglo-Boer War 1899-1902* Professor Pretorius offers the full story in fascinating detail. There are substantial chapters on food supplies and how they were handled during both the early, set-piece phases of the war and what was done in the guerrilla period. Clothing, tents, arms, and ammunition are discussed in detail. In addition to the material requirements, the author delves into the organisational with chapters on discipline and on daily life in camp. The place of religion in their lives, their relationships with each other and their reactions to the experience of battle are revealingly portrayed. The more difficult topics of the way in which black Africans were treated and of the way in which the commandos related to women are tackled with balance and warmth; under Pretorius's hand these people emerge as whole characters. It is thrilling to have verbatim accounts of the advance of the British at the battle of Modder River as seen through Boer eyes, and an invaluable counter-balance to the British accounts we are used to. It is even more valuable to read the chapter devoted to The Bitter End having become acquainted with the variety and diversity of Boer opinions in previous chapters and then to examine the impact of approaching surrender on the men who had fought so long. In both Britain and South Africa the mythology of the commandos has been powerful. In Britain the romanticised will o' the whisp legend of de Wet and his like obscured the military reality and in South Africa the aura of noble, heroic fighters for freedom covered up their human flaws and laid a foundation for for a pernicious doctrine of racial superiority. Neither image survives the clear picture painted by Professor Pretorius and no serious student of the war, be their interest military or social, can neglect this book.
Martin Marix Evans

The Penguin Book
of War – Great
Military Writings,
John Keegan, 1999
Penguin 0 670
85299 5 £25.00,.
The Vintage Book
of War Stories,
Edited by Sebastian
Faulks and Jorg
Hensgen £7.99

These two anthologies, each fascinating in its own right, are even more interesting read together. John Keegan has made, in the words of his publisher's blurb, 'a collection of warrior testimony ... the authentic voice of the combatant'. Sebastian Faulks and Jorg Hensgen took their extracts from 20th century war fiction - 'What all have in common is an appreciation of the intensity of the war experience and what it has meant in this century'.

Keegan opens with a highly elegant, eight-page essay tracing the development of the contrasting military traditions of European and non-European civilisation, the latter 'alternative form of warfare ... the obverse of the "gentleman's war" around which European civilisation had organised itself since the Greeks defined its central values ...' His 'warrior words' cover two and a half millennia from the Peloponnesian Wars of the 5th century to the Gulf war in 1990. Brief introductions place the extracts in context and connect with the opening essay. Not quite all of the 82 pieces are the authentic voices of combatants, but the few exceptions justify their inclusion. The anthology is punctuated by a dozen poems, significant combatant voices amongst them, which are left to speak eloquently for themselves.

In his equally elegant introduction Faulkes

reflects on the nature of the war novel and its evolution through the century 'as the wars themselves became different'. Of the 40 authors represented, at least 15 were in combat so their writing records authentic experience, even if the voice is fictional. This is where reading the books together gets really interesting! The fullest overlap probably where two of the century's great writers describe some of the personal experience of war that informed their novels, Catch 22 and Slaughterhouse-Five (Faulkes confesses to cheating here, in the best interests of the reader). Getting on for half the novelists had first-hand experience of combat and though only Siegfried Sassoon features in both anthologies, as poet in one, as novelist and novelist's character in the other, several more could have.

So what makes the writing different? Part of the answer may have been best expressed by Henry Clifford VC of the Rifle Brigade, writing home from the Crimea in 1854, '... you must understand that it is only in my power to tell you what I see and hear ...' (Keegan p.187) Then read Tim O'Brien, Vietnam veteran, on 'How to tell a true war story'(Faulkes p.306). Or look, for example, at the matter-of-fact and terse descriptions of the most lethally violent episodes of the Napoleonic Wars (Sergeant William Lawrence at Badajoz, Captain Roeder in the retreat from Moscow) or World War I (Compton Mackenzie at Gallipoli, Robert Graves and Erwin Rommel in France). Contrast novelists' accounts of comparable scenes in World War I (Erich Remarque, William Boyd) and World War II (James Jones, Joseph Heller). At the level of his immediate surroundings the combatant actually sees or remembers far less than the creative artist does in the eye of imagination. But, in the best writing as represented in both these collections, both voices, the warrior's and the novelist's, are true. Now read on!
William Shepherd

The Negro's Civil War: How American Blacks Felt and Acted During the War for the Union James M. McPherson (Ballantine Books, New York, NY, $10.00)

Much has been written about the Civil War and years preceding the war and how slaves and freemen were affected. Some people erroneously believe the war was started to free them, whereas the Emancipation Proclamation came almost two years after it began, and we realize somewhat the motivations and actions of the black soldiers and sailors in it, but little has been written as a comprehensive history of black Americans in this period until McPherson turned his incisive pen to the subject. His is a familiar name, and his history of the Civil War, *Battle Cry of Freedom*, is perhaps the third most read and collected (after Catton and Foote) account of the war. Just as all white Americans were not of a common mind about the war, neither were all black Americans. Using diaries, newpaper articles, letters, speeches, and contemporary publications, McPherson has winnowed the words of slaves, intellectuals, preachers, soldiers, teachers, and professionals of color to reveal a complex and varied tapestry of the social, political, and military history of black Americans during the Civil War years. Many novices feel that the Negro was almost a bystander in this war which was so crucial to his well-being, and McPherson's book clearly illustrates how involved in the issues of emancipation and secession blacks were as men of their time. The book reveals attitudes toward the coming war, contrasts attitudes of Northern and Southern blacks, deals with the acceptance of black military units, the Confederate decision to raise a Negro army, the Negro's attitude toward Lincoln, and the prospects Negroes saw for themselves at war's end. This book is a well-crafted read on a topic of which many of us are only lightly versed, and it sheds much-needed light on an era of American history which may force all Americans to reevaluate their notions of that time. It is a necessary and readable addition to every bookshelf.
Carl Smith

An Intimate History of Killing: Face-to-Face Killing in Twentieth-Century Warfare by Joanna Bourke, Granta Books, 1999, ISBN 1 86207 214 0, £25.00

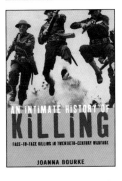

As Joanna Bourke points out in the introduction to her thought-provoking book, the place of actual killing in modern military history is often marginalised. The main focus military history is on the strategic or tactical level, when death enters into it, it is in the form of butcher's bills and the like, the aim of this title as explicitly stated is '[to] put killing back into military history'. This is not done for any voyeuristic purpose, rather, the author argues that the very nature of 20th-century warfare encouraged killing without brutalisation, that ordinary civilians were persuaded to take an active pleasure in combat.

This argument is based around the study of three 20th-century conflicts; the First World War, the Second World War and the Vietnam War, arguably the three most influential conflicts of the century, and certainly the ones for which the most evidence survives. Through the use of the personal accounts of combatants, principally letters and diaries, and secondary material such as training manuals, magazines and contemporary films. The picture that emerges from this collection of evidence holds certain similarities with Niall Ferguson's recent publication on the First World War, *The Pity of War* (1998), namely that individual soldiers were not being coerced into fighting, rather that they were seeking to emulate an heroic ideal propagated by the media of the day. Also revealing is the extent to which a large proportion of the combatants appear to have been willing not only to take their place in the front line, but also to claim full responsibility for their actions and even profess an enjoyment in face-to-face warfare (it is interesting that in a century of warfare dominated by ever increasing tech-nological reliance, in particular the devastating killing power of artillery, the bayonet has remained central both in military training manuals and for the ordinary soldier).

This book is a thought provoking study that should stir up a good deal of debate. It skilfully re-introduces killing and the nature of personal combat into a genre which has neglected its vital role, as emphasised by a padre in First World War France quoted in the book, 'The soldier's business is to kill the enemy … and he only tries to avoid being killed for the sake of being efficient.'
Marcus Cowper

Grant Wins The War James R. Arnold (John R. Wiley & Sons, 605 Third Ave., New York, NY 10158-0012, Tel (202) 850-6000, $17.95)

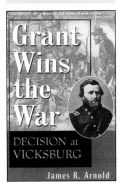

Arnold is no stranger to Osprey readers, having most recently penned the *Gettysburg* Order of Battle series with his wife. *Grant Wins the War* outlines the strategy that General Grant used to bring about the end of the river war, and then to fight his way through the Wilderness, Cold Harbor, and Spotsylvania to accept Robert E. Lee's surrender at Appomattox. The thread of leadership that Grant knotted into a rope to drag the ungelled Union army of early war days to the fighting machine it was at the end of the war runs throughout the book, showing how strategy evolved and solidified with each new experience. Here was the general Lincoln had sought, the man who could win the war for union. From the Red River campaign, through Vicksburg, and then on to Northern Virginia. Arnold presents this case in a factual manner, each incident pushing ahead to an inevitable conclusion which seems so clear to the reader. In vivid prose and with well-researched detail Arnold brings the man and the events to life, giving the book the feeling of being drawn from contemporary headlines. He brings together not only the army, but the navy's side of this campaign and in a nice appendix gives an informative order of battle, identifying the units of both sides, if not all commanding officers, present. For a well-written, insightful, and page-turning account of the Vicksburg campaign which together with Gettysburg turned the tide of the American Civil War, read this book.
Carl Smith

The Hall Handbook of the Anglo-Boer War Darrell Hall, edited by Fransjohan Pretorius and Gilbert Torlage, University of Natal Press, Hardcover £32.50 ISBN 0 86980 943 1, Paperback £25 ISBN 0 86980 949 0,

Major Darrell D. Hall, the outstanding authority on the armies and weapons of the Boer War, died on 11 November 1996. At that time he had just delivered the first draft of his new reference book to his publishers, and now, with the assistance of Professor Pretorius of the University of Pretoria and Gilbert Torlage of Pietermaritzburg and with contributions from Bill Guest, Paul Thompson, Steve Watt, Ken Gillings, Johan Wassermann and Pam McFadden, the work has been brought to a triumphant completion. The authority of these authors is immense and the richness and detail of the book gives full scope to their knowledge. The forces involved – Boer burghers and professional soldiers, the British Army and the Royal Navy – are listed in useful detail. There are technical details of the characteristics of the various artillery pieces, potted biographies of the leading characters and descriptions of the organisation of the forces and the ranks of the officers. The conduct of the war itself is described succinctly, with deployments of Boer forces and strengths usefully summarised. A chapter gives the citations for all awards of the Victoria Cross and another deals with casualties and medical services, including a listing by regiment of losses of officers and of men killed or died or wounds, died of disease, wounded, and missing or prisoner. Black, Indian and Coloured participation is described and the chapter on blockhouses and concentration camps includes a chilling list of deaths in each camp, classified into those under and over fifteen years of age. A chapter on transport and guns is followed by a full list of burial places of Imperial troops. In only one respect does the book fall short of the expectations of an enthusiast – the index. Superficially satisfactory, it does not stand up to the test of the eager quest of the ill-informed, athirst for knowledge; too often it was necessary to comb the text for a hidden nugget of crucial value. For anyone needing detailed information, however, the book is far too valuable to allow this single imperfection to get in the way. The publishers accept Visa and Mastercard. E-mail: books@press.unp.ac.za or fax 0331 260 5801.
Martin Marix Evans

Calendar
Shows and Events

29 April–7 May

Italian International Modelling Show and Competition held at Via Roma n, 14-Calenzano, Florence. For further details **Email dguglielmi@iol.it**

6 May

15th UK Toy & Model Show promoted by Plastic Warrior magazine at Queen Charlotte Hall, Parkshott, Richmond, Surrey. **Tel. (0)1483 722778, Fax. (0)1483 772723**

7 May

Victorian Military Fair 2000 at the Victory Services Club, Seymour St, London W2, 10.30am - 4.30pm. For further details **tel. (0)1635 48628**

12–14 May

Canadian Exposition 2000 – The Canadian War Museum Military Modelling National Exposition at Vimy House, 221 Champagne Avenue N, Ottawa, Ontario. **Fax/phone 613 224 6209, Email acpubmsid@igs.net**

14 May

Model Soldier Day hosted by the British Model Soldier Society National Collection at Hatfield House, Hatfield, Hertfordshire. Members free with membership card

27–29 May

Overlord 2000 – The Military Vehicle Trust annual show at Inhams Lane, Denmead Village, nr Portsmouth, Hampshire. **General enquiries** (0)2392 250463

28–29 May

Their Finest Hour – Dunkirk 60th anniversary event staged by English Heritage in association with Osprey Publishing at Dover Castle, Kent, from noon each day. **Information (0)1304 201628**

28–29 May

Hadrian's Wall – The Roman Army Returns, living history staged by English Heritage from noon each day (Sunday, various sites; Monday, Chesters Roman Fort). **Information (0)1434 681379**

1 June

Military Book Show sponsored by Primedia at Chicago Hilton & Towers, Chicago, Ill., 11.00am -3.00pm

10–11 June

Medieval Siege and Joust at Kenilworth Castle, Warwick from noon each day. **Information (0)1926 852078**

10–11 June

Carlisle Castle Through the Ages – Re-enactment and living history event staged by English Heritage, Carlisle, Cumbria from noon each day. **Information (0)1228 591922**

10–12 June

NSW Diplomacy Championships, held on the Queen's Birthday. Contact Craig Sedgwick. **(o) 2 9661 3926, Email craigsed@ozemail.com.au**

11 June

AMA Grand Event at Academy of Model Aeronautics headquarters, Muncie, Ind. **Information (1) 745 287 1256**

18 June

Samurai Theme Day held by White Rose Military Modelling Society with talks by Dr Stephen Turnbull at Leeds Paxton Horticultural Society Hall, 186 Kirkstall Lane, Leeds, 10.00am - 5.30pm. **Contact (0)113 258 1508**

29 June–2 July

Dragoncon gaming convention at Hyatt Regency, Apparel and Merchandise Mart, Atlanta, Ga. **Information (1) 770 909 0115**

13–16 July

Origins Game Expo at Convention Centre, Columbus, Ohio. **Information (1) 425 204 2677**

13–16 July

The 6th Annual HobbyTown USA National Convention at the Hyatt Regency, Reunion, Dallas, Texas. **Contact Bob Wilke (1) 402 434 5065**

19–22 July

IPMS National Convention – International Plastic Modelers Society, USA and North Central Texas Region, Dallas, Texas. **Information (1) 912 922 3918**

20–23 July

Historicon. Lancaster Host Resort, Lancaster, PA. Contact: James E. Thomas Jr. 8314 Sprague Pl., New Carrollton, MD 20784. **Information (1) 301 562 4879 Email: kinqit@aol.com**

27 July–8 Oct

Invasion 1066 – Re-enactment and living history events on the Norman invasion and the battle of Hastings, staged by English Heritage at Battle Abbey and Pevensey Castle, East Sussex, weekends, from noon each day. **Information (0)1424 773972, (0)1323 762604**

10–13 August

GENCON gaming convention at Midwest Express Center, Milwaukee, Wis. **Information (1) 425 204 2677**

12–13 August

History in Action – the largest living history festival in the world, staged by English Heritage, Spitfire sponsored by Osprey Publishing, at Kirby Hall, Northamptonshire, 9.30am - 6.00pm each day. **Information (0)1536 203230**

19–20 August

British Historical Games Society UK Nationals sponsored by Battle Honours at Loughborough University, 10.00am - 5.00pm each day. **Enquiries (0)1372 812132, Email bhgs@netcomuk.co.uk, Website www.bhgs.co.uk**

16–17 September

Colours 2000 Wargames & Modelling Fair at The Hexagon, Reading, Berkshire. **Email t.j.halsall@reading.ac.uk**

14–15 October

The Battle of Hastings, 1066 – Large-scale re-enactment with many other displays, staged by English Heritage, Norman cavalry sponsored by Osprey Publishing, at Battle Abbey, East Sussex from noon each day. **Information (0)1424 773972. English Heritage website www.english-heritage.org.uk**

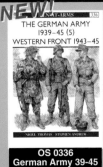

Lone Star
©1999 Don Troiani

"LONE STAR"

Antietam • September 17, 1862

Courage! The 1st Texas valiantly followed the faded silk of their "Lone Star" banner into Miller's cornfield. Only 40 of the 226 men that went in that day walked back out.

Britain's new American Civil War range features the Art of War series, with miniature figures inspired by the artwork of renowned American Civil War artist Don Troiani. The six piece "Lone Star" set is available now and limited to only 5,000 sets.

This new range of figures is meticulously detailed down to the belt buckles, buttons, and regimental flags. Each miniature figure is about 2½ inches tall or 1/32 scale, cast in metal and hand painted in a connoisseur finish.

**TOY SOLDIERS SINCE 1893...
WE'RE HISTORY!**

Ertl Collectibles™

U.S.A. - Britains Ltd., C/O Ertl Collectibles
Hwys 136 and 20,
P.O. Box 500, Dyersville, IA 52040-0500

U.K. - Britains Petite Ltd.,
Falcon Road, Exeter EX2 7LB
Tel: 01392 445434 Fax: 01392 445933

To find your local retailer
call Tel: 1-800-553-4886

Retailers interested in carrying this
line please call Tel: 1-800-872-3785